MEN IN PRIMARY EDUCATION

Mike Keys

MEN IN PRIMARY EDUCATION

Challenging Gender Stereotypes in Schools

S Sage

3rd Floor
HYLO
103–105 Bunhill Row
London, EC1Y 8LZ
UK

2455 Teller Road
Thousand Oaks
California 91320

10th Floor, Emaar Capital Tower
2 MG Road, Sikanderpur, Sector 26
Gurugram, Haryana – 122002
India

8 Marina View Suite 43-053
Asia Square Tower 1
Singapore 018960

Editor: James Clark
Editorial assistant: Harry Dixon
Production editor: Nicola Marshall
Marketing manager: Lucy Sofroniou
Cover design: Sheila Tong
Typeset by: C&M Digitals (P) Ltd, Chennai, India
Printed in the UK

Library of Congress Control Number: 2025945452

British Library Cataloguing in Publication data

A catalogue record for this book is available from the British Library

ISBN 978-1-5296-8518-3
ISBN 978-1-5296-8517-6 (pbk)

CONTENTS

ABOUT THE AUTHOR

Mike Keys is a primary teacher and assistant headteacher with more than 17 years of classroom experience. He has taught in schools across Hertfordshire, Nottinghamshire and South Yorkshire, as well as spending time teaching at an English language college in Western Australia. Alongside his teaching role, he has a particular interest in developing teachers and shaping school curricula. In 2020, with his colleague Matt Withers, he co-founded Men Teach Primary, a social media network created to build a global support network for men to share and celebrate their passion for primary teaching.

INTRODUCTION

It was February 2020, and my wife had just returned from work. She was exhausted. As a GP, her days were becoming increasingly challenging. More patients than usual were coming in, ill and anxious, and colleagues were expressing growing concern about how fast this new virus was spreading and how serious it could become. Trying to lighten the mood, I said something unhelpful like, 'It'll all be fine'. She didn't smile. Instead, she shook her head and said, 'This is going to get really bad, very quickly.' Coming from her, someone not prone to exaggeration, it felt ominous.

In my school, whispers of uncertainty had also begun to weave through the corridors. They were still light-hearted in tone, but worry was growing day by day. Within weeks, the reality of the COVID-19 pandemic became clear, as harrowing footage from Italian hospitals and news of school closures around the world filled the headlines. What was once a distant concern in another country was now beginning to feel closer to home.

As I collected the children from the playground during this period, I could feel the growing anxiety among parents during drop-off. Their conversations were filled with 'What-ifs' and 'Did you hear'. At a parents' meeting a few weeks earlier, one dad had half-joked about whether he should shake my hand after returning from a ski trip in France. We shared a laugh, but the underlying tension was hard to ignore. Inside the staff room, speculation continued. Cups of coffee were cradled nervously as everyone discussed the latest news updates, and some of us even became overnight epidemiology experts. Yet, despite the worry, staff remained determined to keep things normal for the children, essentially to 'keep calm and carry on'.

As the end of March approached, there was still a sense in parts of the country that it might all blow over. Football matches went ahead, crowds packed into a major horse racing festival and the Prime Minister was joking about shaking hands with hospital patients. However, in our school, staff began to show symptoms of the virus and had to take leave, forcing us to operate with a skeleton crew. Then Prime Minister Boris Johnson's lockdown announcement came. 'From this evening, I must give the British people a very simple instruction: you must stay at home.' It hit me like a tonne of bricks. I'd taken everyday freedoms and privileges for granted for a lifetime and their sudden loss was devastating.

During those initial days trapped at home, adapting to a new routine under silent, sunlit skies felt surreal. The streets were deserted, except for queues outside my local Marks & Spencer's, where people stood masked and metres apart, like a scene from a dystopian film. To support my wife's surgery, friends delivered spare PPE, quickly leaving it outside the front door and dashing off as if we lived in a contagion zone.

I tried to keep myself busy. Arts and crafts with my own children. 10,000 steps each day around the garden with a podcast on. And I think I even attempted to bake a banana loaf.

With schools on the cusp of the Easter holidays, there was a brief respite to gather our thoughts and plan. But plan for what exactly? None of us were really sure. Up until that point, my concept of remote learning was what children living on Scottish islands did. However, over the following months, 'You're still on mute' became a refrain we'd come to know all too well. And during this time of crisis, it was great to see families able to rely on the very institutions they trusted the most – schools. The lengths to which many colleagues went to support their communities, from distributing meals door-to-door, to setting up online classrooms, was nothing short of inspiring.

At my school, we grappled with how to support our pupils academically and emotionally, despite the chaos unfolding across the globe. Matt, who had been my Year 6 teaching partner the year before (until he 'abandoned' me to teach Year 2), suggested we lift spirits with some light-hearted video challenges. Matt was the creative energy behind these ideas, always finding ways to inject fun and boost morale. So, we started short contests: the *Haka*, the masked reader and our version of Wimbledon. A small group of staff even remade Peter Kay's *Amarillo* video with Matt as Kay himself – but the less said about that one, the better. The challenge that really took off was 'Join the Chain' – our attempt at a freestyle football video set to upbeat Brazilian samba music. We were far from polished professionals, but this video captured the heart, humour and spirit of our school. Once shared online, it unexpectedly went viral. Sports personalities were retweeting it and news stations picked it up as a feel-good pandemic story. Our little school had its fifteen minutes of fame!

Now, you might be wondering what football videos have to do with the topic of this book. For Matt, it sparked something. He saw how powerful social media could be in spreading ideas and inspiration; so, one evening, I got an intriguing text from him: 'I wanted your advice with something...'. He told me he had just set up a new Twitter group called Men Teach Primary, a space for male educators to connect, share stories and support one another. It had already gained a fair bit of momentum in just a few short days. Matt asked if I would like to collaborate on this venture with him but I was hesitant. I'd only dabbled on Twitter before, mostly to check out great teaching ideas and resources, but I didn't really know how to use it properly. More importantly, I was worried about how some people would interpret the group's aims. The name, 'Men Teach Primary', felt a little precarious, as if it might be misunderstood and labelled as something it wasn't. But Matt is persuasive. As we kept talking about the potential of this platform to spotlight the hidden stories of male teachers, I realised this was an opportunity to build a supportive community during a time of isolation.

In those early months, our group was small but passionate. We connected with teachers working in diverse settings, from tiny rural schools to large urban academies and those teaching internationally. Their enthusiasm shone through as they shared the joys and challenges of guiding children's growth and development. It was exciting to provide a platform for these stories. The conversations were open and welcoming; we weren't aiming to create an exclusive men's club, but to build a network open to everyone.

We held meaningful discussions with groups like Diverse Educators and the Global Equality Collective. And we had the privilege of speaking to inspirational voices in education, such as Dame Alison Peacock, CEO of the Chartered College for Teaching, and renowned educator and keynote speaker, Richard Gerver. His advice, to always lead with positivity in how we framed our mission, stuck with us. From these conversations, the three core aims of Men Teach Primary emerged:

1   To inspire the next generation of male primary teachers.
2   To celebrate and amplify their voices.
3   To empower school staff to challenge gender stereotypes in education.

To live up to these aims, Matt and I launched a blog for male teachers to share their personal stories in their own words. And the responses were incredible: from one male teacher, who moved from working 'on the bins' to thriving in a primary classroom, to another who wrote 'The ballad of a teaching assistant taking cover!', each contribution reflected the richness and range of experiences that bring men into teaching. Alongside amplifying these voices, we spoke on podcasts and collaborated with 'Get into Teaching' to promote the joy of primary and inspire others to join the profession.

As the pandemic went on, our small group grew, as both male and female teachers continued to swap stories and reassure one another. However, after a couple of years of juggling the demands of teaching and family life, running the network in a meaningful way became increasingly challenging. The once lively discussions on minor irritations, like men not being allowed to wear shorts during heatwaves, began to feel repetitive. It was at this point that Matt and I agreed that the project had reached its natural endpoint, and we felt a sense of completion.

But then an unexpected opportunity came our way: the idea of turning our experiences – and the stories we had gathered – into a book. Initially, we were reluctant as we had always seen ourselves as more of a platform for others' stories rather than storytellers in our own right. Moreover, the prospect of writing a book was daunting. Was there something worth saying? Were we the right people to say it? Imposter syndrome was alive and kicking! But the more we thought about it, the more we realised that the story of men in primary teaching was worth sharing and worthy of deeper discussion.

So what is this book about? It's an exploration of the key questions in the story:

•   Why do so few men choose the profession?
•   What does their presence – or absence – mean for schools, for children and for society?
•   What can we do to challenge stereotypes and make primary teaching a career of choice for more men?

While research examining these subjects exists, the information is scattered and hard to find. This book is a way of bringing that information together and adding my perspective as a serving teacher to the conversation. The overall ambition is to give readers the knowledge and context to better understand the story of men in primary and to show that it isn't just a job for some – it's a job for everyone. For teachers, leaders and policymakers, the book goes beyond the surface-level discussions we often see and shines a light on the deeper issues at play. And maybe, just maybe, it will land in the hands of a few young men wondering if they belong in the classroom and help them to see that they do.

PART I

SETTING THE SCENE

1

DOES TEACHER GENDER MATTER?

'My motivation to teach goes back to my year four teacher, Mr Penny. I hated school up until that point, but he helped me see how fun and exciting learning was, and I always sort of thought in my head, I'd quite like to be a teacher like him'.

(Tom Griffiths, primary school teacher, Men Teach Primary, 2020)

WHO WERE THE TEACHERS THAT SHAPED US?

Think back to your primary school days. Picture the classrooms, the playgrounds and the teachers who shaped your early education. Who stands out in your memories? Maybe it's the teacher who turned you into a reader. Or the one who convinced you to audition for the school play, even when you didn't think you were good enough. Perhaps it is the teacher who regularly checked in with you when you were going through a tough time at home.

My own school journey started at the tail end of the 1980s in a primary school on the north coast of Northern Ireland. I can still remember the bustling corridors adorned with 'Stranger Danger' and 'Stop, Look and Listen' posters, the little milk bottles stacked in crates by the door, the well-used Haydn Richards textbooks piled on desks, the feeling of joy at watching the TV on wheels entering the classroom or being given the responsibility for controlling the acetate projector during singing assemblies. But most of all, I recall the teachers who left lasting imprints during these formative years. Teachers like Mr R, whose animated storytelling sessions transported our class into other worlds. Or Mrs A, whose nature table (full of stick insects) was the first place to go when I got to school in the morning.

I can still picture each of my classrooms vividly, with packs of recorders teetering on top of sports equipment, still-drying artwork dangling from ceilings, and teachers' desks cluttered with lipstick-stained tea cups. Among these typical memories, I even remember the most unusual of moments. In my first month of reception, in 1988, Margaret Thatcher visited my school as part of a brief tour of the country. The entire place was buzzing as teachers got us to tuck in our shirts, fix our hair and smile. Looking back, I can only imagine the stress for the staff, managing every detail to ensure the visit went smoothly. All I really remember was the overwhelming noise of the helicopter landing on the school football pitch and the sight of Thatcher herself, struggling to protect her hair from the bitter cold waves of wind being propelled in every direction.

But when I think about that day, what really sticks with me isn't the fact that I saw the Prime Minister. It's how my teachers made it feel like just another school day, no matter what was happening around us. And that's the thing about great teachers: they shape you in ways you don't always appreciate at the time. When I look back, it's not just what they taught that stayed with me, but the way they made me feel – safe, excited to learn, like I mattered. And I'm lucky: I have fond memories of every single one, even the headmaster with his old-school manner and the permanent scent of tobacco wafting from his office. They nurtured my creativity and curiosity and instilled self-belief. Of course, I realise that not everyone has such positive experiences of school, and maybe I recall mine through the lens of someone who became a teacher himself – someone who is possibly more forgiving of the quirks and short fuses I encountered along the way.

However, let's now turn the focus to a different aspect of those memories. How many of those teachers who left lasting impressions on your life were men? If you're like most people, you'll find that women vastly outnumber men in your recollections, and there's a good reason for that. The percentage of male primary teachers in the UK has rarely been high in our lifetimes and has stagnated at around 15 per cent of the workforce over the past decade. In the Early Years, it's as low as 2-3 per cent (Department for Education, 2024). But does it really matter whether or not those influential figures were men or women? Quite simply, the answer is no. The qualities that define great teaching are universal; and for decades, women have formed the backbone of primary education, ensuring schools thrive. This book is not about undermining that contribution in any way.

The real question here isn't about whether a teacher's gender matters – it's whether having a more gender-mixed workforce does. Because when framed this way, the implications become clearer. What happens when children rarely see men in nurturing or educational roles? What assumptions do they begin to form about who belongs in the classroom, or who should care for and teach young children? Of course gender doesn't determine who makes a great teacher; but the fact that so few men enter the profession forces us to ask why not? And, perhaps more importantly, to ask whether the imbalance matters enough for us to do something about it?

A FALSE START

Maybe the sense of belonging I felt as a child is part of why I ended up in the classroom. And that feeling has never really left me. Throughout my career, I've felt welcomed, trusted and appreciated. In fact, it has been mostly the women I have worked with who have made me feel like this. Not in any showy way, but in passing comments and small moments we have shared. Some have shared thoughts openly, while others lean in with a hand covering their mouth like a modern-day footballer shielding a secret from the cameras: 'We could do with a few more men in this place. Don't tell anyone I said that!' These weren't comments made to undermine their brilliant female colleagues. They were about something human: a desire for balance; a team with different experiences, voices and approaches.

Maybe they're also thinking about the wonderful men in their own lives – friends, grandfathers, brothers, husbands, partners, fathers and sons. They think, 'You know what? They'd make fantastic primary teachers.' These men might bring their love of history or science experiments or their enthusiasm for sports and outdoor activities into the classroom. They could lead engaging storytelling sessions or bring new energy to music and arts, all of which adds more voices to the conversation. These offhand comments from colleagues remind us that the call for more men in primary teaching isn't just theoretical. It's something real, felt by those working in our schools.

And so, when I first sat down to start this book, I *thought* I knew what I was doing: the case for more male primary teachers. It felt reasonably straightforward to answer. And early on in the writing process, I thought I'd nailed it. My first draft of this chapter was full of all the buzzwords: 'diversity, representation and inclusion', 'reflecting society', 'broadening perspectives'. It felt satisfying to put the words down, like I'd ticked the right boxes. But then I started reading more, digging into research about men in primary education, and it all got much more confusing. I was experiencing the Dunning Kruger Effect, to full effect, and languishing in the Valley of Despair.

When I came back to the writing months later, it honestly read like word salad. It might have sounded convincing with a Morgan Freeman voiceover, paired with images of children smiling in classrooms. Or with shots of men in tweed blazers and waistcoats standing defiantly on desks, lightbulb moments galore, making learning look like something straight out of an inspirational film. But in black and white on the page? It was too lightweight.

Eventually, I realised something. The question of why we need more men in primary teaching isn't just about finding a stronger argument; it is about building a picture of what it actually means to be a man teaching children. What's it like? What are the pressures? The myths? The rewards? The misconceptions? And over time, these have become the core ideas that hold this book together. They're not revolutionary ideas, but when brought together, they help us see this bigger picture.

1 We Must Start With the Men Already Teaching

Before we talk about how to get more men into primary teaching, we need to spend time listening to the ones who are already here. Not just because they're doing the job day in, day out, but because their stories tell us something important. They show us that men who teach aren't the same. Some are calm and gentle; others are energetic and loud. Some find their passion in teaching the foundations of reading and maths, while others thrive in outdoor learning environments. Their reasons for teaching are just as varied. For some it's a lifelong ambition and for others it's a career change. In Chapters 2 and 3, you'll meet some of these men. We look at who they are, what motivates them, and what they bring to the role because, if we're serious about improving gender balance, we have to listen to them first.

2 We Need to Challenge the Idea that Teaching is Still seen as Women's Work

Most readers probably don't hold this view, but that doesn't mean it's gone; and this belief quietly shapes who applies, how they're treated and how they're perceived. Chapter 7 looks at the gendered assumptions built into society. Chapter 8 takes us into the history of men in primary education and shows where these ideas came from. These chapters are essential for understanding why the imbalance persists.

But when the workforce is more balanced, those old perceptions can start to shift. In one of my previous schools, having both men and women on staff meant children saw teachers taking on all kinds of roles: men leading phonics sessions and women coaching football. It helped break down assumptions about what men and women 'should' be doing, inside and outside the classroom. So, when children grow up in schools where men and women take on a range of roles, they learn that caring, teaching and leading aren't defined by gender. Without that sort of visibility, stereotypes can take hold early. We know from research that by the age of seven, girls are *nine times* more likely than boys to say they'd like to be a teacher (Davies, 2020). It doesn't take a genius to see why that might be.

3 We Need to See How Wider Recruitment Issues Compound the Gender Gap

Challenging the perception that teaching is 'women's work' is only part of the picture. Even if we shift how the role is seen, there are still bigger forces at play. In Chapter 4, we look at the broader structural issues (like status, pay and working conditions) that push both men and women away from primary teaching. These challenges are universal, but they add an extra barrier for men, especially in a society where teaching young children still isn't seen as a 'manly' choice.

4 We Shouldn't Settle for Just any Man

The goal isn't simply to increase the number of men. It's to attract men who genuinely want to teach. We want men who are good at it, who understand the responsibility that comes with the role, and who are in it for the right reasons. A female colleague once joked with me that the problem with male primary teachers is they tend to be either brilliant or dreadful, with not much in between. I've never quite forgotten that line. Because behind the humour is the reality that representation alone is not enough.

We don't need more men who see teaching as a stepping stone or a stop-gap. And while financial incentives might get men through the door, they don't always keep them there. What we need is men who know what they're signing up for, who value the craft of teaching, and who are willing to build their knowledge of how children learn and what makes them tick. The kind of men who love children's literature, who spend time shaping curriculum and who bring richness to the daily lives of children. Men who rise through the ranks without losing sight of the classroom. We need men who are credible.

5 We Need to Listen to Women Too

The story of men in primary doesn't exist in isolation. It's interconnected with the story of women, who have carried this profession for generations, and who still face real barriers, especially when it comes to leadership and career progression. That context matters. As does the reality that men in primary often benefit from being in the minority. That doesn't mean that men don't face challenges, but they also experience perks: faster promotion and novelty status for example. Male teachers need to be aware of both realities and that starts by listening. Listening to the women they work alongside and understanding the discomfort some of them feel when they see men fast-tracked through the system. Chapter 11 examines this in more detail because for men to thrive in primary education, they need women to be on board, and that means recognising that this story isn't all about them.

6 We Need to Stop Recruiting Men as a Way of 'Fixing' Problems

One of the oldest arguments for having more men in primary schools is that they'll solve the 'boy problem' by raising attainment, improving behaviour and serving as male role models (McDowell, 2022). But that line of thinking is flawed. It assumes all boys need the same thing and that men are specially designed to provide it for them. Chapter 9 explores where these arguments come from, why they persist and how they oversimplify the real value that men bring to the classroom.

7 We Must Never Underestimate the Cost of Stigma

Even when men enter teaching for the right reasons, their presence can be misunderstood. Chapter 10 looks at the emotional toll of this. From being viewed with suspicion, to feeling pressure to be a certain kind of man. Some are pushed towards disciplinarian roles while others find their gentleness questioned. These experiences don't just affect wellbeing – they push men out of the profession. Understanding these challenges is crucial if we want men to stay in the job and thrive.

8 We Still Need to Explain Why Men Deserve Attention

Even with all of this in mind, some people will wonder why we need to focus on men at all. It's a fair question, because men, as a group, are not typically disadvantaged in wider society. They have a voice, they have influence and they don't face the same systemic barriers that other underrepresented groups do. So, if we're talking about diversifying the workforce further, shouldn't our focus be on groups who face greater challenges in accessing and progressing in the profession?

Take women in leadership, for example. According to the Department for Education (DfE) workforce census, 2024, women make up around 76 per cent of teachers in England, yet they are under-represented in senior roles, holding only 70 per cent of leadership roles. Despite the progress made here in recent years, there's substantial room for improvement. And when we look at ethnic diversity, the gap is even bigger. While around 17 per cent of teachers come from ethnic minority backgrounds, representation in leadership roles is much lower, ranging between 8 and 10 per cent, depending on the group. These figures highlight why efforts to improve representation need to be wide-ranging. While the Men Teach Primary (MTP) network advocates for more men in primary education, we've always seen this as one piece in the growing anthology of building a diverse and inclusive workforce. It's not about putting one group's needs above another's: it's about ensuring teaching is open to everyone.

SO WHERE DOES THAT LEAVE US?

All of these ideas feed into the bigger question we started with: why do we need more men in primary teaching? But rather than trying to answer it too early (or too simply) this book builds up the evidence first. By the time we reach Chapter 12, we'll have considered the motivations, the history and the challenges. We'll have seen the data, heard the stories and considered the impact. Only then can we return to that original question with the clarity it deserves.

Now that we've set the stage, it's time to meet the cast. The next chapter will introduce you to the voices of male primary teachers. Real people with their own motivations and experiences. Their stories will give us a deeper understanding of the fulfilment that teaching offers.

Time to Reflect 1.1

1   How many of your primary school teachers were men? Did teacher gender matter to your experience as a student?

2   Did you feel a sense of belonging in school? Can you recall times when you, or other children, might not have felt fully included? What role did teachers play in shaping those feelings, positively or negatively?

3   In your view, is focusing on male representation in primary worth the effort? Do you think a broader focus on diversity would be more impactful for education?

REFERENCES

Davies, J. (2020). 'Why we must recruit more men into the early years – and how we can do it'. Early Years Alliance. Available at: www.eyalliance.org.uk/why-we-must-recruit-more-men-early-years-%E2%80%94%C2%A0and-how-we-can-do-it (accessed 4 May 2025).

Department for Education. (2025). 'School workforce in England: Reporting year 2024'. Available at: https://explore-education-statistics.service.gov.uk/find-statistics/school-workforce-in-england/2024 (accessed 19 November 2025).

Department for Education. (2025). 'School workforce in England: Reporting year 2024'. Available at: https://explore-education-statistics.service.gov.uk/find-statistics/school-workforce-in-england/2024 (accessed 19 November 2025).

Department for Education. (2024). 'School workforce in England: November 2023'. Available at: https://explore-education-statistics.service.gov.uk/find-statistics/school-workforce-in-england (accessed 4 May 2025).

McDowell, J. (2022). 'Performing discipline in UK primary school classrooms: challenging essentialist beliefs about teacher gender'. In J. McDowell (ed.), *De-gendering Gendered Occupations: Analysing Professional Discourse* (pp. 158–82). Routledge. https://doi.org/10.4324/9781003159674-9

Men Teach Primary. (2020). 'Why I became a primary teacher – Tom Griffiths' [Video, 25 August]. YouTube. Available at: https://www.youtube.com/watch?v=JL3VQLZw7SI (accessed 4 May 2025).

2
WHO ARE THE MEN TEACHING PRIMARY?

We just need to see men reading story books. We need to see men being silly.
We need to see men dancing and singing in assembly. That's what we need as a
society, and I couldn't recommend teaching more.

(Blair Minchin, primary school teacher, Men Teach Primary, 2020b)

INTRODUCTION

As a young child, I loved story time, especially books by Janet and Alan Ahlberg.
Each Peach Pear Plum and *Burglar Bill* were firm favourites, but one book, *Mr Tick the
Teacher*, always stood out. In it, Mr Tick is the only teacher in a small village school
with six children – all his own. One day, he learns that an inspector is paying a visit
with the intention of shutting down schools with low student numbers. Panic sets
in, but Mr Tick is not one to give up easily. With no time to lose, he and his children
devise a cunning plan. They decide to change outfits for different lessons. One
moment they're in PE kit, the next they're handing out sheet music for a singing
class, followed by dramatic costumes for a theatre lesson. All to keep up the facade
that the school is full of enthusiastic pupils. Mrs. Tick, ever the supportive partner,
plays the role of school secretary and cook. When the inspector arrives, everywhere
he looks, there are 'students' engaged in enthusiastic learning. He's thoroughly
impressed and just like that, thanks to some out-of-the-box thinking, the school
stays open.

On the surface, this is a very silly story about one family's quest to keep their tiny
school open through the art of deception. But something about it has always stuck with
me. Was it the sense of devotion? Or the multidimensional role that teachers play? It
has taken me years to realise exactly why that book resonated with me so much. It is
because, in many ways, it was the story of my family.

WHERE IT ALL BEGAN

My grandfather was the first man in primary teaching that I knew. But to me, he was just Granda. By the time I was born, he was at the end of a long career as a primary headteacher. But in those earlier years, as the head of small rural schools in County Antrim, he wasn't just running the school – he *was* the school. He was often the only class teacher, responsible for every child's education, including his own four children. My mum and her siblings sat in his class, learning alongside their neighbours and friends.

Teaching, for him, was a vocation in the truest sense of the word. He was a clever man – so he told me many times. Coming from a working-class background, at secondary school, he and his siblings scored some of the highest maths marks in the country. Those qualifications could have opened other doors, but it was always going to be teaching for him. He spent his career in schools where many children were destined for a life of farming or manual labour, but he made sure they experienced an enriching curriculum. Every child could play classical music on the recorder. When the Irish weather allowed, lessons took place outside. And in the winter, he read them the classics.

Three of his children – my mum included – became teachers themselves. My uncle went into acting. To this day, they all talk about their primary school days with huge affection. And I suppose that's why *Mr Tick the Teacher* always felt special to me: the small village school, the deep-rooted sense of responsibility and the idea of a whole family bound together by education. It wasn't just a story. It was real life.

And teaching wasn't something my family were able to leave behind at the school gates. It was a big part of our daily life. It shaped conversations, influenced routines and found its way into pretty much every Sunday lunch. Most weekends, a mix of family members would gather, depending on who was visiting. The day usually started with church, followed by a long walk on the beach, and then back to my grandparents' house for a roast dinner. My grandfather would cook while conversations would bounce around the dinner table. The men would discuss the highlights from *Match of the Day* while the women dissected the latest storylines from *EastEnders* and *Coronation Street*.

Once lunch was eaten, the conversation inevitably turned to school. I would listen intently as family members shared tales from their respective schools, both primary and secondary, and the intensity of the job was palpable. They were worn down by the unreasonable demands of parents and leadership, endless piles of marking and an ever-growing list of admin tasks. In hindsight, they were likely close to what we'd now call 'burnout', though the term wasn't widely used back then. Instead, 'absolutely knackered' was the common refrain. Around the table, it was not unusual for one of the teachers to turn to me and say, 'Whatever you do, don't go into teaching'.

Yet, despite the obvious exhaustion etched across their faces, a feeling of fulfilment managed to permeate those stories. Even the most tiring days seemed to be punctuated with enough moments to make it all worthwhile. Whether championing the arts, writing school plays or helping to bring together divided communities, these were the achievements that helped to reinvigorate depleted energy stores. Far outweighing frustrations with paperwork was the satisfaction of making a difference. Just as Mr. Tick and his family exhausted every creative tactic for their small school, the teachers in my family did everything they could for the greater good of the children in their care.

The dedication I saw around the dinner table is the same commitment that many teachers show today. Yet that commitment exists alongside growing pressures. For example, Carpenter (2023) revealed that 93 per cent of educators reported feeling stressed at least once a week. In fact, education was ranked as the most high-pressure career path compared to fields like financial services and insurance. I am sure educators will not be shocked by this data, coming in the same year as multiple national teacher strikes. I know first-hand the difficulties we face in education, and while the future may hold improvements, the negativity surrounding the profession remains one of the biggest barriers to recruitment.

Like many, I've been caught in the cycle of frustration that often comes with teaching and have even considered leaving the profession at times. But despite the difficulties, there are countless reasons to stay. Yes, there's plenty to complain about, but even more to celebrate. It's crucial that we take time to acknowledge why we keep going. For those of us in schools, the pride we feel in our work should never be overshadowed by the challenges. So, that's why I'm going to ground this book in the positive aspects of the profession and the universal reasons teachers choose it in the first place.

FROM CONNECTIONS TO TESTIMONIES

In early 2020, the Men Teach Primary network launched on social media without a plan. Our initial focus was building connections and finding common ground with fellow teachers during the challenging days of the first COVID-19 lockdown. To expand our network and foster engagement, we introduced #MTPMonday and posed the big questions of the day:

- If you could have any superpower, what would it be?
- What's your favourite movie snack of choice?
- What is your favourite British biscuit?

From uncovering whether someone belonged to Team Wagon Wheel or Team Bourbon Cream, it became a safe space for people to connect and participate in light-hearted debates. Scrolling through some of those old threads now, it is hard not to cringe, but ultimately, these harmless chats created a sense of camaraderie for some of us during these tough times. But as the weeks went on, we felt a need for something more. They only scratched the surface of the rich experiences within the teaching community; and with Twitter's character limit, interactions remained too fleeting.

As the network grew, there felt a genuine need to share more. Specifically, we wanted to share the personal stories of men teaching in primary. So, on one otherwise unmemorable Monday, we simply put out a call for contributions. I wouldn't say the floodgates opened;

however, plenty of interest trickled in over the next few days, and our inbox welcomed its first story, a story that would set the tone for the many testimonies that followed.

ANDREW'S STORY

> Teaching was never the plan. I wanted to be a writer or a musician. I wanted to be famous. It makes me laugh to think of this now, because I have been a primary school teacher for 20 years and I love my job. I have taught everything from Y1 to Y6; I have climbed the ladder to headship and I've climbed back down again and returned to the classroom. The last few years in the classroom have been the happiest ones of my career.
>
> (Rough, 2020)

Andrew's journey shared the twists and turns that a teaching career can take, shaped by aspirations, challenges, and ultimately, the pursuit of personal happiness. Initially drawn to teaching almost by chance, Andrew's passion grew as he encountered an inspiring Deputy Head, who embodied the ideal blend of leadership and hands-on teaching: 'That is what I want to be'. Beginning in a challenging school in Feltham, Andrew sought to be a positive male role model in Key Stage 1, recognising the scarcity of men in those formative years. He was comfortable in a predominantly female environment and saw two paths to professional fulfilment: climbing the leadership ladder or becoming an Advanced Skills Teacher.

Andrew quickly ascended to the role of Deputy Head, relishing the status and responsibility but struggling with the demands of what felt like two full-time jobs. His leap to headship two years later, though initially exciting, proved lonely and exhausting. The administrative burdens overshadowed the joy of teaching.

> So I sat back and reflected on that eternal question that had haunted me throughout my career: 'What next?' I had a young family, I was doing a job that I mostly found stressful or boring, and I was beginning to have anxiety attacks because I found most days extremely stressful, and I realised that if this continued, then I would stop being able to do my job well. What had I always loved throughout my career? Teaching. The day-to-day with the kids, the building up of relationships and the sense of pride when you see the children you teach grow and develop.
>
> (Rough, 2020)

Andrew made the decision to take on a teaching role in Year 6, which marked the beginning of his happiest years in education. His guiding principle became, 'Do what makes you happy', and his story is a reminder that success in teaching isn't always about climbing the leadership ladder – it's about finding where you truly belong. One of the acknowledged advantages of being a man in primary education, as I'll explore in Chapter 11, is the higher likelihood of being fast-tracked into leadership. But Andrew's story challenges that idea. His choice shows that promotion isn't always the right path, and stepping back isn't the same as stepping down. It's about choosing the role that brings the most fulfilment. In a profession where leadership can be seen as the ultimate goal, his decision is a reminder that staying in the classroom can be just as valuable.

BUILDING MOMENTUM

Over the following months, the blogs kept coming and featured diverse voices ranging from an ex-Rugby League professional (Cording, 2020) and an ex-Royal Navy medic (Sibbald, 2020) to a stand-up comedian. The latter contains one of my favourite reflections because it captured the essence of what we were hoping to share: 'What I am certain of, though, is that I love doing what I do. I still have an audience when I read the class a book and they are far more preferable an audience to two hundred slightly inebriated hecklers in a comedy club or eight hundred holidaymakers who couldn't care less whether you were there or not so long as the lager is cheap' (Aldredge, 2020). Each story shared on the MTP platform proved to be unique. Some poignant, some laugh-out-loud funny, and some a combination of both.

Throughout this period, Matt was becoming increasingly skilled in creating video content and keen to sustain momentum and enhance accessibility, so the Men Teach Primary YouTube channel was born. Initially, we were concerned that the loss of anonymity in videos might frighten off potential contributors but, contrary to this worry, the response was nothing short of remarkable. The trickle of interest for the blog now turned into a stream, with many men in primary and early years expressing a desire for their 'Mr. DeMille' moment. An enthusiastic community of storytellers emerged, eager to share their experiences and insights.

ADAM'S STORY

Adam's story (Men Teach Primary, 2020a), sent to us early in our project, was not just impactful but stopped me in my tracks. His video gained a high number of views because it's authentic, vulnerable and deeply inspirational. In it, Adam shares his journey of struggling with identity and societal expectations growing up. The emotional moments in the video, especially when he discusses the absence of a role model during his primary years to affirm his individuality, make it a compelling watch. In Adam's own words:

> I was motivated to go into primary school for a very personal reason. I'm an
> openly gay, proud man, and it meant growing up, I was very different,
> especially different to a lot of the boys around me… I struggled with fitting in,
> and society tells you that as a boy, you should behave in certain ways.

I never really had a male role model to tell me it was okay. So, I'm trying to be that male role model, that visible alternative form of masculinity, to say that this version is valid as much as that version is valid… I always tell my class to embrace the weird, be yourself, and, as RuPaul says, if you can't love yourself, how are you gonna love someone else.

(Men Teach Primary, 2020a)

For all the children in Adam's class, especially those who may feel different, his story challenges outdated beliefs about masculinity and shows a male teacher being fully himself. His class is a special place for his children, where individuality is not just accepted but genuinely valued. And this goes to show the transformative impact that a dedicated teacher can have through creating a place where every version of oneself is not just validated but celebrated. To me, this sums up the essence of primary education. Classrooms can be places where teachers like Adam play a pivotal role in shaping not only the academic side but also nurturing the emotional well-being of their students.

Would I recommend teaching? That's like asking if you would recommend Mary Berry bake you a cake! Yes, I would recommend teaching. It's the best job in the world. There's no better feeling than when you've guided this group to achieve such great things. You are changing lives and it's a wonderful experience.

(Men Teach Primary, 2020a)

CAMRON'S STORY

In July 2022, a message of appreciation landed in our inbox. In it, Camron, a primary teacher from Birmingham, thanked us for sharing his blog (Mills, 2022). His story had transcended the digital world, presenting him with a host of unexpected opportunities: Camron had featured on Teachers Talk Radio, spoken at two Multi-Academy Trust conferences, addressed trainee PGCE students, and even became a part of a documentary addressing racism in education. His blog quickly became our most read, and it was a real moment of satisfaction. Not for our accomplishment (all we did was host it), but in the power of storytelling to draw attention to important issues facing some men in teaching.

I still vividly remember reading Camron's story upon first receiving it. After the first read, I read it again. Some stories are so impactful that they take longer to process, and this was one of them. As a Black primary teacher, Camron revealed the challenges of being a minority in the teaching profession. Like so many other blog contributors, his story begins with a transformative experience working abroad. What started as a one-year internship in a school became a six-year stay.

One career-defining event which happened in Thailand was when one of my students competed in an educational English-speaking competition.

The student confidently held her own against students from more affluent schools, including some international schools. My student made it through to the regional stages (one round away from the nationals). The celebration in the school and later in the village was simply mind-blowing! The villagers were amazed that one of their own could achieve so highly and compete with the region's most privileged and most educated. It was at this moment that I knew I wanted to work with disadvantaged children.

(Mills, 2022)

Upon returning to the UK, Camron became immediately aware of the deep-rooted educational disadvantages tied to social class and ethnicity. Citing a report that revealed a 21 per cent lower acceptance rate for Black trainee teachers, he highlighted the under-representation of Black teachers across all career phases (Whittaker 2022).

'It is hard to put into words what it is like to look around you and see so few people that look like you, so few people that understand your lived experiences, so few people to turn to for advice.'

(Mills, 2022)

Camron also reflects on the low expectations he faced, such as being steered toward pastoral roles over academic leadership. Tereshchenko, Bradbury, and Mills (2021) highlight that this is a widespread issue faced by ethnic minority staff, showing that Camron's experience is part of a broader pattern. Alongside these systemic barriers, he also experienced disheartening encounters with parents. One incident involved a parent seeking to relocate their child from Camron's class, stating that their child would be better served by a teacher who, in their words, was 'more like them' – specifically, the white female teacher next door. Another incident, early in his career, took place during his morning runs with a child with social, emotional and mental health needs. Several parents called the school office to raise concerns about 'a big Black man chasing a child around the school field, and the child looks terrified'. It was shocking, but sadly not surprising. In Camron's words: 'For some parents, they may not have seen or spoken to a Black teacher before' (Mills, 2022).

Camron's journey is one of challenging perceptions around race and education. At the time of writing, he had secured the role of deputy head in charge of curriculum, teaching and learning, but for Camron, this was much more than a personal success. Taking on such a role meant that he could be the visible force for good that he desired, smashing stereotypes and inspiring the children in his community. Camron's experiences are hard to hear, but they reveal the often-overlooked barriers that Black teachers face. His story is a reminder of a double absence in primary schools – a shortage of men and an even deeper scarcity of Black male teachers.

EMBRACING INDIVIDUALITY

In all three stories, despite the challenges faced, what stands out is a shared love of teaching. Andrew, Adam and Camron bring different experiences, backgrounds and personalities but all speak passionately about the rewards of working with children; and by sharing these stories, MTP have always wanted to challenge the stereotype that men in teaching can be defined by a single set of characteristics or skills. Just as not every female teacher is an imitation of Miss Honey from *Matilda*, not all male teachers are as boisterous as Mr. Poppy from *Nativity*. Men are far from being a homogenous group. Instead, it's their multiple identities that really enrich the profession.

Becky Francis' 2008 study on male primary teachers revealed just how differently men approach teaching. She notes 'the absurdity in expecting that men teachers would teach, or relate to pupils, in predictable or uniform ways simply on the basis of their "maleness" (Francis, 2008, p.119). For instance, the men studied had contrasting teaching styles, varied approaches to behaviour management and interacted with their pupils in significantly different ways. And knowing this to be true matters, because it shows that we can't make the case for more male teachers by assuming they'll all offer the same thing. What matters is recognising and valuing the different strengths and quirks each person brings to the classroom. As we conclude, it feels right to end with one final reflection that captures what this work is really about.

> I would recommend [primary teaching] to anybody. It would be lovely to see more men in the classroom as there are not enough of us – it's not seen as a very 'manly' job for some reason, but the reality is, it's brilliant… if any men out there are thinking about giving it a go, just go for it. Honestly, it's absolutely brilliant.
>
> (Dave McPartlin, primary school headteacher,
> Men Teach Primary, 2020c)

Time to Reflect 2.1

1   Have you ever held assumptions about what male teachers might be like, or noticed colleagues or students that do?
2   Think about the connection between joy and resilience in teaching. What brings you the most joy in your role, and how do you balance it against the challenges?

REFERENCES

Aldredge, S. (2020). 'Cabaret and comedy to the classroom'. Men Teach Primary, 13 August. Available at: https://menteachprimary.wordpress.com/2020/08/13/cabaret-and-comedy-to-the-classroom/ (accessed 5 May 2025).

Carpenter, H. (2023). How stressed are teachers compared with other professions? *Schools Week*, 11 July. Available at: https://schoolsweek.co.uk/how-stressed-are-teachers-compared-with-other-professions/ (accessed 5 May 2025).

Cording, J. (2020). 'From the boot room to the classroom'. Men Teach Primary, 30 May. Available at: https://menteachprimary.wordpress.com/2020/05/30/from-the-boot-room-to-the-classroom/ (accessed 5 May 2025).

Francis, B. (2008). 'Teaching manfully? Exploring gendered subjectivities and power via analysis of men teachers' gender performance'. *Gender and Education*, *20*(2), 109–22. https://doi.org/10.1080/09540250701797226

Men Teach Primary. (2020a). '#MeetTheTeacher: Adam Levick' [Video, 4 September]. YouTube. Available at: www.youtube.com/watch?v=Jfl_PYhC0v0 (accessed 5 May 2025).

Men Teach Primary. (2020b). '#MeetTheTeacher: Blair Minchin' [Video, 14 September]. YouTube. Available at: www.youtube.com/watch?v=vHOQpXUtEDo&t=23s (accessed 10 November 2025).

Men Teach Primary. (2020c). 'Interview with D. McPartlin' [Video, 29 November]. YouTube. Available at: www.youtube.com/watch?v=EdQrw1qyoqU (accessed 5 May 2025).

Mills, C. (2022). 'A Black teacher's journey into primary education'. Men Teach Primary, 7 June. Available at: https://menteachprimary.wordpress.com/2022/06/07/a-black-teachers-journey-into-primary-education/ (accessed 5 May 2025).

Rough, A. (2020). 'Expectations of a male primary school teacher – Classroom to headship and back again!; Men Teach Primary. 22 April. https://menteachprimary.wordpress.com/2020/04/22/example-post-3/ (accessed 10 November 2025)

Sibbald, J. (2020). 'Patients to pupils – Royal Naval medic turned primary teacher'. Men Teach Primary, 27 June. Available at: https://menteachprimary.wordpress.com/2020/06/27/patients-to-pupils-royal-naval-medic-turned-primary-teacher/ (accessed 5 May 2025).

Tereshchenko, A., Bradbury, A., & Mills, M. (2021). 'What makes minority ethnic teachers stay in teaching, or leave?' Policy Briefing from the Centre for Teachers & Teaching Research. UCL Institute of Education. Available at: https://discovery.ucl.ac.uk/id/eprint/10127240/1/What%20makes%20minority%20ethnic%20teachers%20stay%20in%20teaching%20or%20leave.pdf (accessed 5 May 2025).

Whittaker, F. (2022). 'Non-white candidates less likely to get into teacher training'. *Schools Week*, 18 May. Available at: https://schoolsweek.co.uk/non-white-candidates-less-likely-to-get-into-teacher-training/ (accessed 5 May 2025).

3

WHAT MOTIVATES US TO TEACH?

In America, doctors, lawyers, generals, actors, television people and politicians are admired and rewarded. Not teachers. Teaching is the downstairs maid of professions. Teachers are told to use the service door or go around the back. They are congratulated on having ATTO (all that time off). They are spoken of patronisingly and patted, retroactively, on their silvery locks.

(Frank McCourt, *Teacher Man*, 2005, p. 2)

INTRODUCTION

Teaching certainly isn't for everyone. Some days, I'm not even sure it's for me. Those days when half the class hasn't named their work, the Pritt sticks have disappeared or run out (again) and comma splicing is all you can see when you mark the children's work. Or the bone-crushing fatigue that hits at the end of term; marathon over, body done in. But something keeps drawing us teachers back in. A reason we stay, even when it would be easier not to. This chapter is about stepping back and asking: 'What is it that keeps us going?' To answer that, we're starting with our own stories. How did Matt and I end up in the classroom and what's kept us there?

MY STORY

Growing up in a family filled with teachers meant that teaching wasn't just a career choice for me but a constant presence in my upbringing and community. Town outings with my mum and grandfather became impromptu reunions as they constantly bumped into ex-colleagues, parents and former pupils. In a town that relishes a good chat, I remember standing around a lot with arms folded. I was also one of those children who lingered around after school, wandering the empty corridors, or fantasising about being Cantona or Gazza as I walloped a football repeatedly against the goalpost-painted wall in the playground while my mum prepped her classroom for the next day. These experiences laid the groundwork for my journey into primary teaching.

Beyond family connections, another significant factor came from my time in the Boys Brigade during my teenage years. One of the organisation's aims was the development of leadership skills, and the opportunities I had to work with the younger groups during this time struck a chord. I really enjoyed it but kept that to myself. Back in school, once I was in sixth form in the early 2000s, talk of careers began to surface. One day, I had to fill out a computer questionnaire, the kind meant to unlock the mysteries of my future with a dozen or so clicks of the mouse. Even by the standards of the time, the program used was well past its sell-by date. After answering a series of questions about my interests and skills – both of which I was trying to work out at that age – a definitive list of my ideal future careers was produced, printed out on that old fax paper with perforated edges. There was no discussion. It was just handed over with a plea to read it and start making some decisions.

I remember scanning through the list and finding the results rather puzzling. There, in the top five, was 'Librarian'. At the time, I was certainly not an avid reader, but when asked, 'Do you enjoy reading books?' with just a 'yes' or 'no' option, I went with the affirmative. Apparently, this meant that a future immersed in Dewey decimal classification awaited me. Then there was 'Careers Adviser', which was slightly ironic. And then, completely out of the blue, came 'Brewer', a career path that seemed particularly out of place as I hadn't so much as sniffed a pint of beer at that age. Next up was 'Teacher', and at the time, I probably rolled my eyes. I couldn't imagine anything more awful than spending my life in a classroom surrounded by children who had as much interest in learning as I did in becoming a librarian. But even though it looked like a relic of the past, maybe this program knew me better than I knew myself.

Despite spending my young adult years rejecting teaching as a potential career option and adamantly declaring I would never pursue it, the tide began to turn during my time at university. As my degree flashed by in a blur of more socialising than studying, the prospect of teaching suddenly raised its head as a possibility. While some of my peers were making the most of career fairs and visiting graduate schemes, I was too busy sleeping in late or perfecting my Pro Evolution Soccer skills, blissfully letting those options pass me by. As opportunities dwindled, I realised that teaching was not only the career I was familiar with but also, if I was being honest, the job that suited me best. There was never a 180-degree turn; I didn't wake up one morning and decide to become a teacher. However, the thoughts began to take root in my mind. Teaching gradually felt less like a back-up plan and more like the natural next step.

In 2005, a summer with BUNAC (British Universities North America Club) took me to an arts and music camp in upstate New York, which sounded like the perfect setting to nurture any budding teaching or mentoring skills. However, there was a problem. The desired role of camp counsellor was out of reach and I found myself assigned to maintenance – a job for which my skills were laughably inadequate. Within the world of manual labour, I was (and still am) as useful as a chocolate teapot. My incompetence didn't escape the notice of the maintenance team, who quickly relegated me to tasks that required minimal skill, like driving the pick-up truck to the dump and becoming a champion toilet unblocker. I unblocked so many toilets that summer that I earned the nickname 'Plunge Master', complete with a t-shirt to honour my special talent.

Fortunately, these less glamorous duties allowed for unexpected interactions with the campers. Between dump runs and plumbing exploits, I found moments to chat, joke and even sneak into activities when my boss wasn't watching. These light-hearted moments gave me a glimpse of how rewarding it could be to work with young people. So, when I returned home, I started some work experience back in my old primary school and finally accepted that teaching might be for me after all.

MATT'S STORY

After graduating from university, I started my career at Rolls-Royce, taking on a role that brought the prestige and challenge of working for a globally renowned corporation. I spent a lot of my early years travelling: I lived in China, Japan and the United States, jetting off to different cities and managing teams worldwide. Believe it or not, I used to fly to work every week, commuting from San Francisco to San Diego and back. There were lots of emails, lots of phone calls, lots of visitors to meet and greet. Yet, despite the benefits of this jet-setting lifestyle and the thrill of experiencing cultures from around the world, a desire for something different was always in the back of my mind.

After the first five to six years of my career, I realised that climbing the corporate ladder wasn't as fulfilling as I thought it might be. I looked at my seniors and couldn't picture myself in their shoes, decades down the line, confined to their desks. So, my desire for change grew stronger by the day. What I really wanted was something hands-on, something that aligned more closely with my personality and skills.

It was primary teaching that captured my interest. This profession promised not just creativity but also offered a more balanced lifestyle, which was especially appealing as I planned to start a family. Unlike Mike, it was not a particularly familiar career. I didn't have many family members working in education, but as a teenager and young adult, I was involved in coaching local football teams and working at outdoor educational centres. I always felt I had a knack for connecting with children. This background helped solidify my decision to make a leap of faith and transition from one career path to another.

Making the switch was not without its challenges. I left my well-paid job to enter the unfamiliar world of teacher training, enrolling in the Schools Direct programme at Derby University. Managing mortgage payments during this time was tricky, but I was convinced that it was the right decision for the long term. Spending four days a week in a classroom and one at the university was demanding but suited me perfectly.

My first real test as a teacher came during a lesson in Year 2, where I decided to make *papier-mâché* pigs. After weeks of observing and learning, I thought, *I've got this*. It was supposed to be a simple, fun activity related to 'The Three Little Pigs.' The kids and I were excited, but things didn't go as planned. Unfortunately, I used permanent pink paint, which not only ended up on the pigs but all over the children's uniforms as they enthusiastically painted their creations. It was only afterwards that we realised the permanence of the paint, leading to an embarrassing call to parents informing them that new uniforms might be necessary. It was a baptism of fire, a moment when the boardrooms of San Francisco felt a world away. This incident is not only etched in my memory, but taught me the importance of learning on the job and adapting quickly. Schools are such busy environments where no two days are the same. I quickly learned that adaptability and a good sense of humour are so important in this profession.

As time has passed, teaching in various year groups, from Year Two to Year Six, each day brings new discoveries, reaffirming my choice to change careers. The creative aspects of teaching – from arts and crafts to science experiments – allow me to share my enthusiasm and watch as the spark of curiosity ignites in my pupils. Overall, I can confidently say that the shift from the corporate sector to the classroom has been a move into a more fulfilling chapter of my life. It not only aligns with my desire for an engaging career but has also given me a deep sense of accomplishment and purpose in my everyday life.

WHAT MAKES PRIMARY TEACHING SPECIAL?

Now we take a step back to consider what draws so many others to teaching in the first place. In early 2024, the MTP network asked fellow educators, via social media, to share what fuels their passion for primary teaching. The responses highlighted many of the universal rewards: the variety of roles we take on, from storytelling to scientific exploration; the intellectual challenge of adapting lessons to meet every child's needs; and the chance to begin again each September with a new class, new challenges and new ideas. But one theme stood out above all others: the children themselves.

The Joy of Working with Children

The children are at the core of what makes teaching fulfilling. It would be hard to find a teacher who doesn't treasure those breakthroughs when something clicks and you see it on the child's face. And it's not just the academic side that makes the classroom special. It's the random, completely unplanned moments that happen in between. Whether it's a question you weren't expecting or a comment you can't unhear, children have a way of making every day memorable.

I remember during a reflective session with Year 6, as we discussed memorable moments from their time at school, one child announced that his proudest moment was not an academic achievement but finally playing a human in his final year performance after years of only being cast as animals or various forms of vegetation. You probably had to be there, but it triggered such a wave of laughter that we could barely continue. I also remember another child who was supposed to be collecting animal and plant specimens from the school pond for a hands-on classification lesson but ended up falling in, completely submerging himself. Panic was rapidly followed by laughter as he emerged, algae-coated, with a massive grin on his face and his thumb up. We all laughed, and thankfully his parents did too when they found out. There's *always* something different about having a good laugh with children. They love it when they 'break' your teacher facade, when professional barriers temporarily drop and you form deep connections. It's a pretty unbeatable feeling.

And of course, laughter is only part of the story. Beyond the lighter moments, teaching also brings encounters with children who leave a lasting impact on us for different reasons. Among my own collection, one child's story stands out. He was a child who found the mainstream classroom setting overwhelming at times, which could manifest in aggression. His fight-or-flight response was acute, leading to outbursts that could disrupt the calm of any school day, and navigating the year was a journey of learning and growth – not just for him but also for me.

There were times when I reacted less patiently than I should have, but our collective goal was always clear: to ensure his success and well-being. With the support of an incredible teaching assistant and his hugely supportive parents, we made significant progress. The year ended on a positive note, with the child making academic and personal strides that filled us all with pride. However, as with many of our students, we don't always know what happens to them once they move on.

Fast forward to a year later: I was visiting a local secondary school as part of a transition day for my Year 6 class. It came at a point when I had been questioning whether my future lay in education. I had been feeling fairly disillusioned and had made the decision to move schools at the end of the year. Walking the school grounds alone, I spotted *him* heading towards me. He was taller now, but looked awkward in his oversized school blazer. His smile was something I hadn't often seen during his year in my class. He stopped right in front of me and looked me in the eye – something he rarely did back then – and said, 'I hear you're leaving.' I told him it was true and time for a change. He paused and walked forward a few steps. He turned again to respond, 'Whichever school gets you next, they're lucky.'

His words were simple but took me by surprise. At that moment, doubts about what I did for a living were temporarily dispelled. He not only acknowledged the past we shared but also offered encouragement at a time when I least expected it but most needed it. It was a moment of affirmation, and it reminded me that our influence often reaches into the lives of our students in ways we might never fully appreciate until much later. And I suppose this is why I teach. It's these real connections and small transformations that make the work feel worthwhile.

The Lasting Impact of Teachers

Teaching is not just about what children bring to our lives. It's also about the mark we leave on theirs. Every so often, even major celebrities will name a teacher who changed everything for them. For example, in a live concert special in 2021, Adele reconnected with her childhood English teacher, Ms McDonald (ITV News, 2021). Adele told the audience, 'It was just one year, but she got me really into literature. She also did street dance in the canteen... She was so bloody cool, so engaging. She was there, and we knew she cared about us.' When Adele spotted her in the crowd and they embraced on stage, it was a special moment. Similarly, during an episode of the BBC's *One Show* in 2022, actor Will Poulter was visibly moved by a surprise video message from a former maths teacher who had supported him during a difficult time in secondary school. Both examples show how even small gestures of kindness and understanding from teachers can leave a lasting emotional impact.

While it might sound clichéd, the idea of 'making a difference' is a reality. Teachers have the opportunity to guide students onto better paths, affirm their worth and build their resilience and confidence. I would argue that apart from those working in health-care, educators are perhaps the only professionals whose impact can evoke such deep emotional appreciation. Imagine a talk show where a guest bursts into tears upon being reunited, not with a teacher, but with their tax accountant who saved them some money years before; it's unlikely. What teachers do stays with people. Sometimes forever.

And before we get into the depressing numbers and the challenges we face in education, it felt right to start with what brings people into this job in the first place. Because if we want more men to choose primary teaching, we can't just talk about what's going wrong. We have to show what makes it worth it.

REFERENCES

ITV News. (2021). 'Adele has emotional reunion with old schoolteacher during special concert', 22 November. Available at: www.itv.com/news/2021-11-22/adele-has-emotional-reunion-with-old-schoolteacher-during-special-concert (accessed 18 May 2025).

McCourt, F. (2005). *Teacher Man: A Memoir*. New York: Scribner.

4

FACING THE FACTS: WHAT DO THE STATISTICS REVEAL?

They're bigger, they're taller, they're hairier than your average primary teacher. Who are these mysterious beings?

(The One Show, BBC, 2010)*

INTRODUCTION

This chapter serves as our reality check because, despite being a profession packed with opportunities for personal and professional fulfilment, not many men want to do it. And for those who do, quite a high number leave every year. These aren't new revelations, but they do deserve proper attention and, although the statistics don't tell the whole story, they're the best place to start.

THE SAME OLD STORY

To gather the most accurate and up-to-date stats for this book, I began where most modern inquiries do: with a search engine. Typing 'number of male teachers in primary schools' consistently brings up the same headlines, with each publication presenting the scarcity of men as though it were breaking news. I can't imagine readers seeing these and saying, 'Wait, you're telling me there's hardly any men teaching in primary schools? You can't be serious!' Matt and I joke about how there must be a moment every year when journalists check off their list of annual stories and decide it's time for their piece on the lack of men in primary education. It's right up there with predictable headlines like, 'Fuel prices expected to rise again', or, 'Hospital waiting lists hit new highs'.

I remember the first time I conducted this search; it felt like opening a time capsule. The same numbers and concerns kept coming up, along with familiar public opinions that haven't changed much in decades. The articles always contain familiar themes, with headlines that could quickly populate a 'men in teaching' bingo card: 'lack of male role models', 'steady decline', 'poor pay', 'discipline', 'boys are behind'. Year after year, the stories are disturbingly consistent, with each cycle bringing the same old calls for more male teachers. Even the visuals remain unchanged, often reusing the same three or four stock images of smiling men in classrooms. It's almost as if life has three certainties: death, taxes and the low number of men in nursery and primary education.

One particularly memorable moment came when I clicked on a promising link, only to be greeted with a yellow banner warning me that the article was nearly two decades old. The headline? 'Primary schools lack male teachers.' The irony was not lost on me. The issue had remained stagnant while years had rolled by. Even more striking was a clip I discovered on YouTube from a 2010 episode of *The One Show*. At the time, there was a significant push to redirect men from failing industries post-recession into primary education. The presenter opens the segment with the quote at the beginning of the chapter and, following this playful introduction, a man dressed like a bank manager sits awkwardly in a nursery role-play area. At the same time, little children enthusiastically play hairdresser, wielding their brushes right next to his grinning face. Overall, the feature certainly hinted at the individual talents men can bring to teaching, and even concluded with actor Patrick Stewart thanking a primary teacher for inspiring his path into acting. However, like many others, this piece underlined a crucial point. The discussion around men in primary education has been long-standing and remarkably unchanged.

THE STATISTICS

The most recent Department for Education workforce figures (DfE, 2025) show a persistent and significant gender imbalance across the education system in England:

- **Secondary schools**: about 35 per cent of teachers are male – a proportion that has declined steadily since 2010.
- **Primary and nursery schools**: only 14 per cent of teachers are male. That means an estimated 300,000 children attend primary schools with no male teachers at all – The so-called 'No Sirs' schools (Sabey, 2018).
- **Special schools and pupil referral units**: around 24 per cent of teachers are male, a higher proportion that may reflect different perceptions of the role and the working environment.
- **Teaching assistants**: 93 per cent are female across all state schools, meaning that children rarely encounter men in support or pastoral roles either.

The consistency of these findings across various educational stages and regions illustrates the depth of the issue. And it's not just a British problem. A similar internet search of other countries reveals the same story. For instance, a headline from an Australian news article warns: 'Male primary school teacher numbers dropping, will be 'extinct' by 2067, study finds' (Rubinsztein-Dunlop, 2017). In the Republic of Ireland, the proportion of male primary teachers hovers around the 14 per cent mark, and low figures are echoed across the globe. Research from Germany, Vietnam, South Africa and Iceland reveals that the scarcity of male primary school teachers is a global challenge (McDowell, 2023).

A PATTERN BEYOND TEACHING

The low numbers of men in primary is not unique. It's part of a wider trend across professions traditionally seen as 'women's work'. Known collectively as HEED professions – health, education, early years, and domestic roles – these sectors consistently struggle with male representation. For instance, in England, men comprise 10.9 per cent of registered nurses (Forrest, 2023) and 17.3 per cent of registered social workers (Social Work England, 2022). These figures show how traditional gender roles still influence what society sees as 'appropriate' work for men and women. And the lack of progress in these roles is not new. The proportion of male nurses has barely changed in 20 years, while the percentage of men working in early education has seen no increase for a quarter of a century (Gender Diversity Task and Finish Group, 2020).

Although these numbers are probably not surprising, they still paint a grim picture of male representation in HEED professions. Both nursing and social care, like teaching, struggle to recruit enough workers, even though half the population remains an untapped resource. However, societal expectations continue to discourage men from pursuing these roles. While this chapter focuses on the size of the challenge, later, in Chapter 7, I will take a look at how our gendered world impacts professional choices.

TEACHING IN CRISIS

While social barriers clearly play a huge role in the low numbers of men in primary teaching, it would be a mistake to assume that they alone are to blame. Teaching as a profession faces significant challenges that affect all staff, regardless of gender. In the UK, anyone with an ear for education news will know that the recruitment and retention of teachers has been a concern for many years now. I genuinely feel like the profession has been in a state of crisis for the duration of my teaching career, judging by the number of times I've heard about it. A quick internet search for 'teacher recruitment crisis' unveils another seemingly endless stream of negative headlines. Here are just three recent examples from 2024:

- 'DfE on track to miss teacher recruitment targets, again' (Cumiskey, 2024).
- 'The teaching profession is in crisis' (NASUWT, 2024). This article highlights the overwhelming workload and stress levels experienced by teachers, with 73 per cent considering leaving the profession.
- 'MPs told why people don't want to be teachers anymore as recruitment hits crisis levels' (Busby, 2023).

And if proof were needed that the UK has faced a chronic teacher supply issue for a long time, here is another headline from years ago, when the BBC declared:

- 'New teachers: 30% of 2010 intake quit within five years' (Coughlan, 2016).

The National Foundation for Educational Research (NFER) annual report on the teacher labour market confirms that the profession is in a critical state (McLean et al., 2024). In the 2023–24 academic year, secondary teaching recruitment reached only 50 per cent of its target and, while primary recruitment managed slightly better, it still fell significantly short of demand. Retention rates further highlight the fragility of the teaching workforce. In 2021/22, 9.7 per cent of teachers left the profession – equivalent to 40,000 teachers – the highest level since records began in 2010 (House of Commons Education Committee, 2024). Moreover, data from Tes revealed that over a 12-year period, 40,438 state school teachers left within just one year of qualifying (Peirson-Hagger, 2024).

WHAT'S BEHIND THE NUMBERS?

The NFER report highlights that 'teacher pay has not kept pace with average UK earnings over the last decade'. Between 2014 and 2021, teacher salaries on the main scale rose by just 3–5 percent, while wages across the broader economy grew by nearly 8 per cent (Zuccollo, 2022). That might not sound like much of a difference, but when you consider rising living costs, it becomes a real problem. In real terms, experienced teachers' salaries were 12 per cent lower in 2023/24 than they were in 2010/11. Even the 6.5 per cent pay rise in 2023 wasn't enough to catch up. And if teaching is falling behind other professions, it's hard to blame graduates for looking elsewhere. In the USA, the situation is even worse: in 2022, teachers earned 26.4 per cent less than their non-teaching peers – the largest pay gap since 1960 (Allegretto, 2023). While the specific challenges in each country differ, one thing is clear: teaching often fails to offer the financial incentives necessary to attract and retain high-calibre graduates.

Workload, unsurprisingly, remains another substantial barrier. According to the Working lives of teachers and leaders survey (2024), full-time teachers in the UK worked an average of 52.4 hours per week in 2023 – an increase from 51.9 hours in 2022. Leaders fared even worse, averaging 58.2 hours per week (Booth and Dyson, 2024). These figures far exceed the national average for full-time employees in other sectors, showing the intense demands placed on educators. While long hours are not unique to teaching, the profession's combination of workload and responsibility creates a particularly challenging environment.

Nearly half (44 percent) of teachers and leaders in the survey rated their anxiety levels as 'high' the previous day – a figure unchanged from the previous year's findings. The 2019 Trades Union Congress (TUC) report revealed that teachers work more unpaid overtime than any other profession, with primary teachers logging an additional 13 hours per week. In terms of unpaid labour, this puts teaching ahead of high-pressure roles like chief executives, lawyers, and finance managers (Henshaw, 2019).

WHY ARE GRADUATES TURNING AWAY FROM TEACHING?

In my early years of teaching, the situation felt very different. During my training, I remember my tutors emphasising the importance of visiting many schools and working on our CVs to make us stand out as quality candidates because getting a job was tough. Teaching roles attracted a large number of applicants and getting through to the interview stage was a significant achievement. At school, my peers would discuss teaching as a viable career option, and at university, it was seen as a sensible and stable choice – far from a plan B or C. Fast forward to my experiences in recent years, and the landscape has shifted dramatically. Job adverts often go unanswered, creating mounting pressure just to keep classrooms staffed.

This shift raises an important question: why are so many graduates now shunning teaching as a career? Training enrolments are falling far short of targets, as mentioned above, so this makes it crucial to look upstream and investigate what might be going wrong. In 2023, Durham University surveyed 4,500 undergraduates across 53 universities in England to find the answer. What they discovered was fairly definitive. 'For all of the students we surveyed, the biggest deterrent to teaching as a career was that teacher salaries are not high enough' (Gorard and See, 2023).

And future projections don't offer much optimism. The NFER report warns that 'Teacher supply is likely to remain significantly below target for primary schools in coming years, despite falling pupil rolls', even with measures like bursaries and international recruitment (Turner, 2024). Overall, these findings highlight the urgent need for systemic reform. Without addressing pay competitiveness and workload effectively, it is fair to say that the teaching profession will remain in this state of perpetual crisis. And while these challenges affect almost every school, they create an even greater obstacle to increasing male representation. Because ultimately, these universal barriers create an even steeper hill for men to climb, as they sit on top of the gender-specific challenges discussed later in this book. If schools are struggling to attract any teachers, recruiting men becomes even harder. It's virtually impossible to diversify the workforce when vacancies go unfilled and the goal is simply to keep a school running.

Time to Reflect 4.1

In a book of this scope, it's impossible to cover every contributing factor or potential solution in detail. However, these statistics raise a couple of questions that merit further exploration if we are to address the challenges highlighted here more effectively:

(Continued)

---

1 Are men leaving primary teaching for different reasons than women?

The answer is likely yes and no. Workload, pay and lack of promotion opportunities are universal challenges that drive many teachers out. However, women often face additional pressures tied to motherhood, such as poor maternity pay and a lack of flexible working conditions. Women aged 30-39 have been the largest group of teachers leaving the profession every year since 2017 - a group three times larger than men of the same age (Jeffreys, 2024). So, while we have some evidence, the picture is far from clear. Generic explanations for leaving will likely lead to generic solutions, and these may not address the underlying causes for particular groups of teachers.

2 Can we learn lessons from other female-dominated professions?

As we have just seen, fields like nursing and social care face similar struggles with male under-representation. Is there potential for these professions to collaborate, sharing strategies that have worked - or even learning from each other's mistakes? Could a joined-up approach reveal more effective ways to attract and retain men in traditionally female professions?

REFERENCES

Allegretto, S. A. (2023). 'Teacher pay penalty still looms large: trends in teacher wages and compensation through 2022'. Economic Policy Institute. Available at: https://www.epi.org/publication/teacher-pay-in-2022/ (accessed 18 May 2025).

BBC. (2010). *The One Show*, 5 April: 'More men primary school teachers needed - Oughtbridge Primary School' [Video]. YouTube. Available at: www.youtube.com/watch?v=FE2ScyqMpaE (accessed 18 May 2025).

Booth, S., & Dyson, J. (2024). 'Heads and teachers working longer despite workload push'. *Schools Week*, 29 February. Available at: https://schoolsweek.co.uk/heads-and-teachers-working-longer-despite-workload-push/ (accessed 18 May 2025).

Busby, E. (2023). 'MPs told why people don't want to be teachers anymore as recruitment hits crisis levels'. *The Independent*, 15 November. Available at: www.independent.co.uk/news/education/teacher-recruitment-levels-pay-working-b2447630.html (accessed 18 May 2025).

Coughlan, S. (2016). 'New teachers: 30% of 2010 intake quit within five years'. BBC News, 24 October. Available at: https://www.bbc.co.uk/news/education-37750489 (accessed 18 May 2025).

Cumiskey, L. (2024). 'DfE on track to miss teacher recruitment targets, again'. *Schools Week*, 30 March. Available at: https://schoolsweek.co.uk/dfe-on-track-to-miss-teacher-recruitment-targets-again/ (accessed 18 May 2025).

Department for Education. (2025). 'School workforce in England: Reporting year 2024'. Available at: https://explore-education-statistics.service.gov.uk/find-statistics/school-workforce-in-england/2024 (accessed 29 October 2025).

Forrest, B. (2023). 'Men in nursing: Smoke and mirrors'. *British Journal of Nursing*, *32*(5), 234. https://doi.org/10.12968/bjon.2023.32.5.234

Gender Diversity Task and Finish Group. (2020). 'Improving gender balance and increasing diversity in England's early years education workforce'. Department for Education. Available at: https://miteyuk.org/wp-content/uploads/2020/11/gdtfg-final-report.pdf (last accessed 18 May 2025).

Gorard, S., & See, B. H. (2023). 'Why are so many graduates shunning teaching? Pay – but not bonuses – could be the answer'. *The Conversation*, 21 November. Available at: https://theconversation.com/why-are-so-many-graduates-shunning-teaching-pay-but-not-bonuses-could-be-the-answer-216963 (accessed 18 May 2025).

Henshaw, C. (2019). 'Teachers work more unpaid overtime than anyone else'. *Tes Magazine*. 1 March. Available at: www.tes.com/magazine/archive/teachers-work-more-unpaid-overtime-anyone-else (accessed 18 May 2025).

House of Commons Education Committee. (2024). 'Teacher recruitment, training and retention: Second report of session 2023–24' (HC 119). UK Parliament. Available at: https://publications.parliament.uk/pa/cm5804/cmselect/cmeduc/119/report.html (accessed 18 May 2025).

Jeffreys, B. (2024). 'Teacher mums who leave profession fuelling shortages'. BBC News, 2 August. Available at: www.bbc.co.uk/news/articles/c51yzv95wg9o (accessed 18 May 2025).

McDowell, J. (2023). "If you're a male primary teacher, there's a big 'why are you doing that? What is wrong with you?'" Gendered expectations of male primary teachers: The 'double bind'. *Sociology Compass*, *17*(12), e13145. https://doi.org/10.1111/soc4.13145

McLean, D., Worth, J., & Smith, A. (2024). 'Teacher labour market in England: Annual Report 2024'. National Foundation for Educational Research. Available at: https://www.nfer.ac.uk/publications/teacher-labour-market-in-england-annual-report-2024/ (accessed 18 May 2025).

National Association of Schoolmasters Union of Women Teachers (NASUWT). (2024). 'The teaching profession is in crisis'. Available at: https://www.nasuwt.org.uk/article-listing/the-teaching-profession-is-in-crisis.html (accessed 18 May 2025).

Peirson-Hagger, E. (2024). 'The scale of the teacher retention crisis revealed'. *Tes Magazine*, 21 June. Available at: www.tes.com/magazine/analysis/general/teacher-retention-scale-crisis-revealed-dfe-data (accessed 18 May 2025).

Rubinsztein-Dunlop, S. (2017). 'Male primary school teacher numbers dropping, will be 'extinct' by 2067, study finds'. ABC News, 18 September. Available at: www.abc.net.au/news/2017-09-18/male-primary-school-teachers-extinct-in-australia-in-50-years/8956770 (accessed 18 May 2025).

Sabey, R. (2018). 'Over 300,000 pupils are being taught in primary schools without a male teacher'. *The Sun*, 9 December. Available at: www.thesun.co.uk/news/7934730/three-thousand-schools-no-male-teachers/ (accessed 18 May 2025).

Social Work England. (2022). 'Social work in England: Emerging themes'. Available at: www.socialworkengland.org.uk/about/publications/social-work-in-england-emerging-themes/ (accessed 18 May 2025).

Turner, C. (2024). 'Significant' primary teacher shortages likely despite falling rolls'. *Tes Magazine*, 14 May. Available at: www.tes.com/magazine/news/general/significant-primary-teacher-shortages-likely-despite-falling-rolls (accessed 18 May 2025).

Zuccollo, J. (2022). 'Teachers' pay in context'. Education Policy Institute. Available at: https://epi.org.uk/publications-and-research/teachers-pay-in-context/ (accessed 18 May 2025).

5

A WAKE-UP CALL

I don't accept what I call the 'It-is-what-it-is-ology...' 'It is what it is' – five tiny words deadened by defeatism. They carry the frustration that comes when we know something is wrong, but are also convinced that there is nothing to be done to fix it. They allow us to turn away and embrace cynicism too, by rewarding the cynics.

(Alastair Campbell, 2023, p. 121)

INTRODUCTION

In the summer of 2020, following the various blog posts and YouTube stories the MTP network had shared, the *Tes* reached out, inviting us to write an article. We decided that addressing the persistent myths surrounding male primary teachers would be ideal. Fortunately, the response was overwhelmingly positive and it sparked some great discussions across social media comment sections. Here is a flavour of what was said (Reddit, 2020):

- 'I was given a job within a class with 'difficult' boys because the headteacher wanted 'to inject some testosterone into the classroom'. Needless to say, behaviour was no better than it had been in the previous 5 years of the class.'
- 'I must say a lot of my friends and family seem to think that I'm looking for a role as head in the future when really all I want to do is teach.'
- 'I am a nerdy-looking dude who is doing his primary PGCE from Sept, and honestly, I can say the thought of people thinking I'm a pervert almost stopped me from applying at one point.'
- 'I have also had to put up with a fair few 'child molestation' comments, particularly from 'friends' when I first started out in the profession. However, this wasn't particularly helped when my university put on a seminar about the subject which only men were invited to. I refused to go, citing that surely women could be paedophiles as well?'

Despite the support, a few dismissive voices emerged, and true to my nature, these were the comments that captured my attention. I wasn't expecting universal positivity, but the naysayers made me realise two crucial things. First, I just didn't know enough about the issues surrounding men in primary. My knowledge was superficial at best and the article itself didn't say anything new or particularly meaningful. I was certainly not a voice of authority on the topic, so I couldn't debate the more negative responses with much confidence. For example, one reader commented, 'Men and women are different – simples. Read what Jordan Peterson has to say about it.' My response was disappointing: 'OK, thanks for reading – I will check it out.' That was it. I had nothing else to say.

Second, I realised that not everyone shares the same level of interest or positivity about having more men in primary education. Some people hold dismissive or even negative views about the topic, while others are simply indifferent. In hindsight, this should have been obvious. Why would others care as much as we did? At the time, though, we were riding a wave of momentum. The growing network, the blogs and videos that kept coming through, the opportunities to speak to well-known voices in education, and a constant stream of social media positivity, all felt like progress. But in reality, we were stuck in a bit of an echo chamber. Great though it was, this momentum wasn't reaching beyond the people who were already interested or invested in the issue. Without stepping outside this bubble and addressing the wider range of attitudes – from cynicism to apathy – we were never going to make meaningful progress.

WHEN SUPPORT DOESN'T TRANSLATE INTO ACTION

Throughout our teaching careers, Matt and I have met many people who acknowledge the importance of having more men in primary education. The overwhelmingly positive response to our article really highlighted this enthusiasm, with many female educators sharing their experiences about how few male teachers their own children had had, and others discussing the positive working relationships they shared with male colleagues. But positivity alone doesn't lead to progress. In fact, as we continued to expand the MTP network, I started paying closer attention to what people were really saying. Not just the provocative posts on social media but the casual conversations in staffrooms, the side remarks from colleagues and even passing comments from parents.

What follows now are a few of the most common attitudes I've encountered when talking about this topic. You might recognise them from your own school or community – or even in yourself. This isn't about pointing fingers. It's about understanding where people are coming from and thinking about what it might take to move them towards greater support.

Apathy: 'It Is What It Is'

These are the educators who agree that we need a more diverse workforce but don't feel able to do much about it. They might nod along in meetings or sign a petition, but beyond that, they're often too busy to get involved. When you're juggling everything teaching throws at you, there's not much headspace left for anything extra. 'How are we supposed to change something that's always been this way?' they might ask, doubting that new initiatives can really make a difference in a system that feels so stuck in its gendered ways. They just want to focus on what they can control in their own classrooms, so they tend to stay out of wider discussions, often with a sense of resignation: 'You can pour all the energy and money you want into this, but nothing's going to change.'

Short-Termism: 'We Need Bodies in Classrooms'

This perspective is pure pragmatism. 'We just need teachers!' could be their rallying cry, putting the immediate need for staff ahead of the longer-term goal of a more representative workforce. As we saw in Chapter 4, schools are often struggling just to fill positions, let alone achieve improved gender balance. When Matt and I presented to ITT providers as part of a DEI series a few years ago, a representative acknowledged our goals but pointed out the main difficulty: 'Colleges are struggling to fill places full stop', he said, suggesting that our aspirations for gender balance were unrealistic given the broader recruitment crisis.

This is a viewpoint grounded in reality, prioritising the urgent over the ideal. And this sentiment became particularly clear as our own network started to feel the pressures of the national teaching shortages. A couple of years after we launched, the enthusiasm for celebrating and promoting men in primary began to fade, overshadowed by the more pressing need to address the general scarcity of teachers. Some of our earliest supporters were exhausted. Some had even decided to leave teaching altogether. When you're questioning your own future as a teacher, discussions around diversity naturally take a back seat. No one was hostile, but the feeling of being out of touch with the broader context or needing to 'read the room' led us to gradually pull back from focused diversity efforts in favour of showing support for the profession in general.

Cynicism - 'Another Round of Box-Ticking'

Imagine the cynic as the Gene Wilder meme in full Willy Wonka regalia, grinning as if to say, 'Oh, go on, tell me why we need more men?' These are the individuals who often view efforts to increase the number of men with a large dose of scepticism. But this scepticism isn't unfounded. The cynic is often an experienced teacher who's seen plenty of initiatives come and go. They remember past attempts like the government's 'Troops to Teachers' or the drive to recruit men from business after the financial crash. These ultimately fizzled out, with little lasting impact. You can almost hear them say, 'So, bringing in more men is going to make boys learn better, is it?', with the sarcasm barely disguised.

Their doubts are further fuelled by the reality that men in primary often rise to leadership roles more quickly, and not always because of their dedication or competence.

In 2016 it was reported that half of new women primary leaders had been qualified for nine years or more, compared with just six years or less for men (Staufenberg, 2018). And a *Tes* survey from 2021, revealed that 21 per cent of male primary teachers saw themselves as headteachers in the next decade versus just 9 percent of women. Considering this, the cynic's concerns start to make sense. Vivienne Porritt, strategic leader for WomenEd, hit the nail on the head when she said that while it's positive for more men to work in primary education, we must also question 'the support and development that women receive to encourage them to apply to headship' (Lough, 2021).

At the beginning of my career, I remember chatting to colleagues about the challenges of having trainee teachers in your classroom. We discussed the lottery of who you get and the balancing act of giving them space to learn while watching them fail. One teacher recounted her experience with the worst trainee she'd ever had. He never prepared lessons, didn't take advice and always had a ready-made excuse for everything that went wrong. We all nodded in sympathy. Fast forward a few more months, and she walked into the staffroom with a look of disbelief. 'Do you remember that terrible trainee I told you about?', she asked. We nodded again, curious. 'Well, I found out he's now a headteacher, telling people like me how to do my job!' It was the sort of moment where, as a man, you don't quite know where to look.

Maintaining the Status Quo – 'If It's Not Broken, Why Fix It?'

These are the individuals who feel comfortable with the way things are. For some, a primary school environment offers a sense of security and community that they value highly – especially if they've had negative experiences in more male-dominated workplaces. Imagine a teacher (male or female) who once worked in a high-pressure corporate job where competition and traditionally 'masculine' behaviours are the norm. In contrast, the working environment of a primary school may provide a welcome change. Ultimately, there may be concerns that increasing the number of men in the field could shift workplace dynamics too much, potentially introducing elements into the job that they find less appealing.

FROM TESTIMONIES TO RESEARCH

So, after the first couple of years of networking, Matt and I knew that real progress was only possible if we learned more. We needed to know what the research said and we had to explore the psychological dimension in more depth – how people think, feel and respond to the idea of increasing male teachers. Without addressing both areas, any momentum we gained was bound to disappear. But how could we investigate this on a meaningful scale? It felt like an impossible task until one day an email landed in our inbox and we realised the next step was right in front of our eyes the whole time.

REFERENCES

Campbell, A. (2023). *But What Can I Do? Why Politics Has Gone So Wrong, and How You Can Help Fix It*. London: Penguin Books.

Keys, M., & Withers, M. (2020). 'Four myths about male primary teachers'. *Tes Magazine*, 26 July. Available at: www.tes.com/magazine/archive/4-myths-about-male-primary-teachers (accessed 18 May 2025).

Lough, C. (2021). 'Male teachers 'twice as likely to want headship'. *Tes Magazine*, 27 October. Available at: www.tes.com/magazine/news/general/male-teachers-twice-likely-want-headship (accessed 18 May 2025).

Reddit. (2020). '4 myths about male primary teachers' [Online forum post, Redditu/OriginalPosterUsername, 26 July]. Available at: www.reddit.com/r/TeachingUK/comments/hzeqt9/4_myths_about_male_primary_teachers/ (accessed 18 May 2025).

Staufenberg, J. (2018). 'Men get promoted more quickly, and 4 other findings from new school leadership research'. *Schools Week*, 11 April. Available at: https://schoolsweek.co.uk/men-get-promoted-more-quickly-and-4-other-findings-from-new-school-leadership-research/ (accessed 18 May 2025).

6

OUR SURVEY SAYS... WHAT DO EDUCATORS THINK?

> I am writing to your organisation as a representative of the Teacher Diversity Team at the Department for Education... We would be interested in understanding more about your organisation and the work you do.
>
> (DfE, personal communication, 21 November 2022)

INTRODUCTION

The email was a surprise, given that our social media content mostly focused on light-hearted engagement, such as, 'What was your favourite children's TV programme?' Matt and I were fairly sure this wasn't quite the 'work' they were interested in. It turned out they wanted to discuss their department's progress on diversifying the teacher work-force, an issue back in the spotlight after a recent parliamentary debate about increasing the recruitment of male primary school teachers. Knowing that this topic was being taken seriously at a national level was motivating. However, while we'd shared blogs and videos and built a strong community online, we couldn't help but feel like something was missing. Speaking to the DfE was a big deal but we didn't feel like we had anything valuable to share.

We'd spent our first couple of years focusing on building our network and raising awareness. It had been a fun and rewarding time but, if we wanted to contribute mean-ingfully to the bigger conversation, we knew we needed more than anecdotes and enthusiasm. We needed real insight into the challenges around male representation in primary teaching. And then the penny dropped. We'd spent all this time building a diverse pool of educators across the country yet we'd never thought to ask them directly about their views. It felt like a slap-your-forehead moment. Why hadn't we done this already?

So, we carried out a survey with more than 250 education staff from around the country. Although not a formal, academic study, it gave us a wide selection of real views from people working in education today. What follows is a summary of the big questions asked, starting with a question directed specifically at men.

Q1 WHY DID YOU WANT TO BECOME A PRIMARY TEACHER?

We've already spent the first part of this book sharing some of the reasons men are drawn to primary teaching – including our own. The responses to this question give us further insight and help us to start spotting patterns. Back in 1993, researchers Williams and Villemez (1993) investigated male entry and exit in female-dominated jobs. They categorised men's career pathways into 'seekers' (men who choose to work in tradition-ally 'female' fields) and 'finders' (men who discover these roles). Years later, Ruth Simpson (2004) identified a third type – 'settlers' – to describe men who enter teaching after leaving more traditionally 'masculine' roles, noting that those in primary educa-tion often fit this pattern. Most of our respondents did in fact fit this mould, coming to teaching after feeling unfulfilled in other careers:

- 'Career had stalled in another industry and I wanted a new and more interesting job.'
- 'I hated working in law – it was a classic bravado, chauvinistic environment...' 'I didn't like the person I was becoming.'

A significant 'finder' presence also emerged with many men saying they found their way into teaching after realising how much they enjoyed working with children in youth groups, sports clubs or camps:

- 'Camp America showed me I had a knack for working with kids, and after university, it was a natural choice.'
- 'I'd done some rugby training in local primary schools through my rugby club and enjoyed it. Also had volunteered at my mum's school and it went from there.'

The most common reason was the desire to 'make a difference.' Though simple, this phrase repeatedly came up, reflecting a drive for work that feels meaningful and reward-ing. In a profession so often associated with poor pay, this shows a genuine priority shift among some of these men. For them, teaching holds value beyond the salary, by offering a purpose that they found lacking in other careers.

- 'After helping in schools in Afghanistan on several deployments there, I was inspired to help all children to learn and fulfil their potential regardless. I was particularly motivated by seeing girls who would have normally been excluded from education flourish with even a basic level of education.'

- 'Mainly because when I was a child, in the 70s and 80s, male teachers were uncaring, overly strict and far too angry. I want boys (and girls) to see that men care, are supportive and want to help them achieve their goals, as well as providing a positive model.'

Many traced their interest back to childhood influences such as a parent, grandparent or an inspiring teacher:

- 'I grew up with a mum who... became a live-in nanny and then nursery nurse. I honestly think it was in my blood to work with children.'
- 'Because I was inspired by my ONLY male primary teacher as a child.'

What Have We Learned? (Q1)

Matt and I can see ourselves in these stories. He's more of a 'settler'; I'm somewhere between that and a 'finder'. But overall, a clear pattern stood out. Most men don't follow a straight line into teaching. For many, it comes after trying something else first. Often, it is the experience of working with children that pushed them in a new direction. And this feels like something we can act on. If these kinds of hands-on experiences have the power to tip the balance, then maybe we need more of them. Maybe we need more chances for men to see the job up close and realise that it might actually suit them. These responses back up the stories shared in Part 1 and challenge the idea that men simply aren't interested in the job. If anything, they show we might be asking the wrong question: it's not about whether men want to teach; it's about how we help more of them realise that they should.

Q2 WHY DO WE NEED MORE MALE PRIMARY TEACHERS?

We started by simply asking whether primary schools needed more male teachers; 92 per cent agreed. To investigate further, we asked why and three clear reasons emerged.

1 Diversity and Representation

Many said that it was important for a teaching workforce to reflect the community it serves; to have a mix of genders, ethnicities and backgrounds to create an environment where all children can see themselves represented and feel a sense of belonging.

- 'Schools are environments that almost everyone in the population experiences. If this environment is not representative of society, then that is not good enough. If schools continue to be made up of a female-dominated workforce with a general lack of diversity, then the next generation will not see the profession as something for them.'

- 'We need a better cross-representation of our society – from gender to ethnicity and beyond – in all sectors of education. If children can't see themselves represented in their role models, then they're inevitably harder to inspire!'

2 Breaking Gender Stereotypes

For others it was less about numbers and more about what their presence could do to challenge traditional gender roles, particularly the idea that teaching young children is 'women's work'. Many respondents felt that a more balanced workforce would help dismantle this stereotype, encouraging all children to follow their interests without feeling limited by outdated gender expectations.

- 'There is nothing particularly different about male primary school teachers *per se*, but the fact that it isn't seen as a "normal" career for men needs to change.
- It will make others realise that primary is an important stage of education and not just "women's work".'

3 Role Models

This was by far the most common reason. Many respondents talked about the value of male teachers as role models – especially for boys – and the importance of children seeing men in nurturing roles.

- 'Children need good male role models. We had lots of children without a dad in their life.'
- 'Positive male role models are important, particularly in areas like my school with massive social problems, crime and high deprivation.'
- 'I think it is important for children, particularly young boys, to see men in the role of a teacher. It shows boys that the pursuit of education and knowledge is intrinsically good. Male teachers can act as role models for young boys, especially those who have been immersed in toxic masculinity.'

What Have We Learned? (Q2)

This question shows some of the most widely held beliefs about why male teachers matter. But it is important to ask whether they all hold up under scrutiny. Later in the book, especially in Chapter 9, I'll take a closer look at these common narratives, such as the need for male disciplinarians or the idea that boys do better with male teachers, and ask whether these arguments help or hinder progress. Then, in Chapter 12, we'll return to the central question to provide a fuller, more nuanced case for why more men might be needed in primary teaching.

Additionally, some responses raised concerns that are worth returning to later. For example, one person commented, 'Primary teaching is best, in my opinion, with females due to their nurturing nature', reflecting a belief that women *are* naturally better suited to the job. Others shared views that highlighted different priorities or frustrations, such as 'targeting a specific demographic is a race to the bottom', or that we should focus more on 'supporting the retention of non-white and non-straight trainees'. Some felt men are uniquely able to connect with boys, while others argued, 'It's about the best person for the job, not their gender.' These comments are important because they reveal how, even within education, assumptions about gender roles and 'natural' abilities still run deep. And they show exactly why we need to look more closely at where those beliefs come from, which is what we do in Chapter 7.

Q3 WHAT IS STOPPING MEN FROM ENTERING PRIMARY TEACHING?

For this question, we provided a few common reasons, two of which are universal to teachers as a whole – pay and conditions and perceived low status – and two that are more male-specific – lack of representation and social stigma. The order of the responses said a lot. Over one in three chose social stigma as the primary barrier. Pay and conditions followed (about a quarter), then perceived low status (about a fifth) and lack of representation (roughly one in eight). But numbers only tell part of the story, so we also asked people to expand on their choices.

1 Social Stigma

Comments revealed deep discomfort with how some people still view men working with young children.

- 'Having seen male EYFS teachers being called 'paedophiles' by uneducated parents... stigma is a real barrier, particularly in early years teaching.'
- 'I've had negative reactions from parents when they realise they have a male teacher. I'm instantly some kind of threat.'
- 'I play Sunday league football, and all of my teammates can't comprehend teaching kids. The idea of changing kids who have wet themselves, singing songs, and teaching things like dance is met with laughter and pity.'

This level of fear reflects what Ruth Simpson found (2004: 23). In her study, male teachers said they felt 'considerable anxiety' about the reactions of male friends, with some reporting actual ridicule or a sense of paranoia around what was being said behind their backs. Similarly, Kimmel (1994) argued that men feel constant pressure to prove their manliness, and jobs like primary teaching are problematic because they do not conform to a masculine ideal. As a result, many men avoid these roles altogether.

2 Workload and Conditions

This was highlighted as a major deterrent to both entering and staying in the profession. Even if the desire to teach was there, the demands of the job make it too challenging for many.

- 'I left teaching due to the extreme workload. Despite being in a friendly, supportive school, I was averaging 70-hour weeks. Now, with a family, this is just not sustainable.'

3 Social Isolation

Although not as popular, some men suggested that there could be a feeling of loneliness attached to being the only man in the building.

- 'I think for many men, working in a female-dominated industry is challenging. It's hard to form social connections, to feel understood and accepted at times, and to find your place in the workplace.'

This point also reminded me of a social media conversation our network was once 'tagged' in, where a young male teacher expressed feeling lonely as the only man in his school and asked for advice. His request was quickly shut down with comments like, 'You do know it's okay to be friends with women?' It was uncomfortable to read because, for some men, the difficulty of connecting socially in a female-dominated profession can feel like a deal-breaker when considering teaching as a long-term career.

What Have We Learned? (Q3)

These responses confirm what we looked at in Chapter 4. Men face a double challenge. Like all teachers, they're affected by pay, workload and status, but layered on top of that are the fears of being judged, being misunderstood or just not fitting in. The fact that social stigma came out as the biggest barrier says a lot. For some men, it's not just about job satisfaction. It's about whether they feel safe, welcome or even trusted in the role. That's a huge ask for any profession. We'll come back to this in Chapter 10 when we look at stigma more closely, but if we want to tackle it properly, we first need to understand where these attitudes come from – and that's exactly what Chapter 7 is about.

Q4 HOW HELPFUL IS THE IDEA OF MALE TEACHERS AS ROLE MODELS?

The idea of men as role models is one of the most common arguments for why we need more male teachers, particularly in primary. But when we asked educators what they thought of this idea, the responses revealed a surprising level of variation. For some, male role models are essential. For others, it's more complicated. Overall, three distinct themes came through.

1 Male Teachers as Father Figures

Some educators see male teachers as filling a kind of surrogate father role, especially in communities where many children don't have any consistent male figure in their lives. Male teachers could therefore fill this void, providing a model of care and calm strength.

- 'Boys from broken homes or from families where the male figure is not a positive influence need to see that there is another way to act and conduct themselves.'
- 'It's important for boys who do not have a good male role model at home, however, female teachers are often just as good a role model for boys.'

2 A Narrow Definition of What Men are For

Many responses were more cautious and worried that the 'role model' label would simplify the role of men in primary schools. They felt it risked pigeonholing men in primary schools as disciplinarians or leaders, rather than simply recognising them as good teachers.

- 'In primary, the role model can sometimes mean that being a male teacher equals headship, and I'm not convinced that's always the most helpful.'
- 'It can be limiting and often an excuse for placing a man in UKS2 or promoting unjustifiably to leadership positions or to manage behaviour.'

3 All Teachers as Role Models

An equally strong theme was the belief that all teachers serve as role models because they all have the power to positively influence children. And while having men in primary education is valuable, the assumption that male teachers are automatically the 'right' role models for boys can feel too simplistic.

- 'A role model should not be gendered. Good role models are good role models.'
- 'You never hear it the other way, with female teachers being held up as role models for wayward girls.'
- 'Not helpful as it disempowers women as role models for boys and implies that all men are of a singular personality type.'

What Have We Learned? (Q4)

The role model concept holds a lot of emotional weight. I have lost count of the number of times I have heard it used in the debate over the lack of male primary teachers. But these responses show just how complicated it can be. If we push it too hard, we risk narrowing what male teachers are allowed to be and put unfair pressure on them to represent something beyond their control. We also risk overlooking the fact that all teachers can be role models, therefore hugely devaluing the role female teachers play. This discussion continues in Chapter 8, where we look at the history behind this idea and where it came from. In Chapter 9, we consider the role model angle from a recruitment perspective. And in Chapter 12, we come back to this concept again, not to dismiss it, but to explore how it could be reframed in a more useful and inclusive way.

Q5 WHAT CHALLENGES DO MALE PRIMARY TEACHERS FACE IN SCHOOL?

Before we move into the next section, it's worth saying that I'm not sharing this next part in search of sympathy. The aim here is just to raise awareness. While the previous question focused on what stops men from entering teaching, this one asks what challenges male teachers face once they're in the job. For many respondents, the answer was simply 'None'. This is a reassuring sign that, in many schools, male staff feel included and valued. Still, as in any profession, there are misunderstandings and occasional frustrations, and a fair number of men shared their experiences of these. Here are the most common challenges, grouped by theme.

1 Social Isolation

- 'I worked at one school where I was one of only two male teachers. It felt very isolating to work in that environment. I had no one I could easily connect with socially.'
- 'It can be quite lonely – it's hard to bond with colleagues when you're the token bloke. Gatherings of staff beyond the obligatory Christmas do often don't include me because they're, in essence, a "girl's night".'
- 'Being the only male in a school can be draining – gender expectations (lifting everything) and not being able to join in all conversations with colleagues.'

2 Stereotypes and Gendered Expectations

- 'Expectation that I want to teach in UKS2 and to lead PE.'
- 'There's a continual assumption that because I'm a man, I must want to be a head teacher, or as a man, I don't need family time.'
- 'I'm always seen as the disciplinarian, always the "bad cop", and expected to run the school football club. I detest most sports.'

3 Sexism

- 'Sexist jokes like "can't multi-task", "he wouldn't understand – he's a bloke" and the presumption that I'll easily get (and actually want) promotions into leadership because I'm male.'
- 'I was once told by a colleague that I'd been given my role because of my gender and not any skill I may have.'
- 'There was a female teacher who had a mug with "I hate men" on it, and "All men are bastards". Can't imagine a man would get away with that. There are regular negative comments about men that seem innocuous and sometimes humorous. Again if men made similar comments we'd be strung up.'

4 Safeguarding Stigmas and Parental Concerns

- 'Parent of a child who was going into my class the next September went directly to SLT [senior leadership team] to state how unsafe it would be for her daughter to have a male teacher. The language she used was so vile that SLT felt like they had no choice but to move her to another class for my protection.'
- 'Challenges around managing children who want to hug or sit on your lap. Never have done this ever, but women do it and it's considered "maternal", yet considered inappropriate if a male did it.'

5 Physical Tasks

- 'Expectation to do all the lifting in school, to sort problems such as taps leaking.'
- 'I'm the one called to do heavy lifting jobs and general DIY tasks around the school. There's a perception that male teachers are always the "muscle".'

What Have We Learned? (Q5)

As expected, the responses show a mixed picture of men in primary teaching. While most reported no significant issues, others shared school-specific challenges, suggesting that the culture within each institution can make all the difference. I couldn't help but smile at the comments about being the go-to 'muscle' for lifting and DIY tasks. Personally, I'd love to be considered the 'muscle' at my school, but it's unlikely. I've also always enjoyed light-hearted banter with colleagues and have rarely encountered anything that felt mean-spirited. I used to work with a teaching assistant who occasionally asked me when I was going to get a 'real job', and I found it hilarious. For me, those moments are part of the camaraderie of the workplace, but as the responses show, it's not the same for everyone. For some men, certain comments and behaviours can tip into genuine hurdles. Sexism, safeguarding stigmas, or being pigeonholed into roles like disciplinarian or sports coach are more serious. These can alienate or exhaust teachers who might otherwise thrive.

This chapter serves as a bit of a linchpin for the book. Looking back to that moment where we realised we needed to hear directly from the profession turned out to be a good call. These responses have given us a way to organise what matters and where to go next as we move onto the barriers, the assumptions and the impact those things have, and what we can actually do about it.

REFERENCES

Kimmel, M. S. (1994). 'Masculinity as homophobia: Fear, shame, and silence in the construction of gender identity'. In H. Brod & M. Kaufman (eds.), *Theorizing Masculinities* (pp. 119–41). Thousand Oaks, CA: Sage Publications.

Simpson, R. (2004). 'Masculinity at work: The experiences of men in female-dominated occupations'. *Work, Employment and Society*, 18(2), 349–68. https://doi.org/10.1177/09500172004042773

Williams, L. S., & Villemez, W. J. (1993). 'Seekers and finders: male entry and exit in female-dominated jobs'. In C. L. Williams (ed.) *Seekers and finders: Male Entry and Exit in Female-dominated Jobs* (Vol. 3, pp. 64–90). Thousand Oaks, CA: Sage Publications. https://doi.org/10.4135/9781483326559

PART II

EXPLORING THE MAIN THEMES

7

OUR GENDERED WORLD: THE REAL VILLAIN?

There is a multitude of interconnected barriers that prevent men from entering primary teaching including the low status and low pay, the homophobic comments, and the slurs of being a sexual predator. Arguably all the issues may be caused by one major factor: society's attitudes to work roles and gender.

(Joanne McDowell, 2023: 15)

INTRODUCTION

Gender is a huge concept, layered with history, science and deeply held beliefs about what it means to be male or female. And while the conversation about gender inequality has often (and rightly) focused on the barriers women face, the impact of gendered expectations on men gets far less attention. This chapter asks what role gender really plays in the low number of men entering the profession.

To make sense of it all, I started by listening to podcasts: gender constructs, societal norms, cultural expectations, socialisation processes, sex differences, cognitive biases, job segregation and biological theories. The list of technical vocabulary seemed never-ending, and it was easy to emerge from the rabbit hole of research more confused than when I entered. But the more I learned, the more one thing stood out. How we behave, the decisions we make and the opportunities we believe are open to us, are all deeply influenced by our gendered world. And nowhere is this more obvious than in the way we think about who belongs in a primary school classroom.

WHAT DO WE MEAN BY A GENDERED WORLD?

Jules Daulby (2019) explains it well: 'If something is gendered, we attribute certain characteristics to it that are not biological, for example, assuming women are fragile or imagining the man in the room is in charge.' And this isn't just about obvious stereotypes like 'blue is for boys' and 'pink is for girls': it starts far earlier, often before a child is even born. I'm sure the majority of parents don't set out to treat boys and girls differently, but Emily Kane's (2012) research shows that many do. In interviews with prospective parents, she found that gendered expectations often appeared even before birth. Men wanted sons they could teach sports to, while women imagined buying dolls and dressing up daughters. Sociologist Barbara Rothman (1986) also discovered that mothers who know they're expecting a boy often describe their baby's movements as 'vigorous' or 'strong', while girls don't get the same labels. In contrast, when the sex was unknown, no differences were reported.

And once a baby is born, gendered attitudes don't take long to creep in. On 11 June 1986, the night Gary Lineker scored a hat-trick against Poland in the World Cup, Neuroscientist Gina Rippon gave birth to her second daughter. That evening, eight out of the nine babies born on her ward were named Gary. Rippon recalls standing with another mum as the calm of the ward was broken by two screaming babies. A 'blue-wrapped Gary' was handed over to his parents with the praise, 'What a cracking pair of lungs'. Meanwhile, Rippon's own daughter, making the exact same noise, was handed over with a frown and the comment, 'She's the noisiest of the lot – not very ladylike' (Robson, 2019). Hearing this story brought back my own memory of the birth of my first daughter. After hours (and eventually days) of labour, my wife was exhausted with the lack of progress and we had no real blueprint for what was normal. In an attempt to reassure us, the midwife said, 'Don't worry, you know what girls are like – always late doing their hair and make-up.' So there it was. My daughter hadn't even been born, and already she'd had her first taste of our gendered world.

These subtle (and not so subtle) differences in how we describe and treat boys and girls add up over time. The toys we give them, the language we use and the behaviours we praise or discourage, all reinforces ideas about who they are and who they're meant to be. As science journalist Melissa Hogenboom (2021) explains, 'These initial divisions may seem innocent, but over time, our gendered worlds have lasting effects on how children grow up to understand themselves and the choices they make.' So now we'll look at how gender inequality plays out across society, how it affects men as well as women, and how even in the most progressive countries, the old expectations still remain.

PROGRESS AND RESISTANCE

You might think that with years of effort to break stereotypes and promote gender equality, the problems associated with gender-based inequalities are becoming a thing of the past. But the truth is, they really aren't. Kane argues that gender remains a powerful social structure that 'limits opportunity, restricts individual potential, and distributes social resources unequally' (2012: 4). In fact, the World Economic Forum's 'Global Gender Gap Report' (2024) estimates that achieving gender parity is still 134 years away. This is a shocking statistic, particularly when we know just how important it is to fight for.

Financially speaking, McKinsey & Company estimate that achieving gender balance in the workplace could add US$28 trillion to global GDP, which is more than the combined GDPs of the United States and China (Woetzel et al., 2015).

The effects of gender inequality are most acutely felt by women. They face disparities in educational opportunities, endure the persistent gender wage gap, shoulder disproportionate household and childcare responsibilities, and are far more likely to experience sexual assault and domestic violence (Leonard, 2021). However, there is growing evidence of progress in certain areas.

- The number of women entering STEM (Science, Technology, Engineering and Maths) careers has grown significantly, doubling to over one million in the UK within the last decade (Institution of Engineering and Technology, 2024). Initiatives like Girls Who Code have already served over half a million girls, with more than 50 per cent coming from historically under-represented groups. And they're on track to close the gender gap in entry-level tech jobs by 2030 (Girls Who Code, 2022).
- In UK politics, female representation has risen significantly. In 1918, the first woman was elected to Parliament. Fast forward 100 years, and in the 2024 general election, 40 per cent of all MPs elected were women (Allen, 2024).
- In the world of sport, the popularity of women's football has exploded over recent years. Known in England as the 'Lioness Effect', the national women's team has inspired a movement. Between 2020 and 2024, the number of girls playing football in schools doubled – an increase of more than 129,000 participants (Sanders & Samuels, 2024).

The efforts that have led to these successes recognise that gender equality has never started from a level playing field. Historically, men and women have had unequal access to opportunities. These examples also show that when government action, workplace policies and collective momentum come together, real change is possible. However, many barriers remain, which is why true gender equality is still such a distant goal. For instance, a 2018 report investigating workplace equity in STEM found that, although there are more women in the workforce, gender bias is common. Amongst a list of demoralising statistics, it was revealed that half of all women in STEM reported experiencing some form of unfairness at work, whether being thought of as less capable, passed over for promotions, or side-lined for important projects (Shuster, 2024).

WHERE DO MEN FIT INTO THE GENDER EQUALITY CONVERSATION?

Gendered barriers impact men too. Social expectations about what it means to 'be a man' often limit emotional expression, discourage nurturing roles, and lead to damaging stereotypes about men's suitability for certain professions (Kane, 2012: 5-6). For many men, the gender equality discussion is rarely about access to leadership positions or high-paying jobs. Instead, the challenge is about whether they feel able to step into roles traditionally seen as 'women's work'. Of course, this isn't true for all men. Race, sexuality and class also still affect who gets what opportunities and who doesn't. But when it comes to the HEED professions, such as nursing and early education (fields I discussed in Chapter 4), societal expectations about what men 'should' do remains one of the biggest barriers to entry.

Iceland offers an interesting case study of these gendered barriers in action. For the 14th year in a row, it has topped the table for gender equality, being the only country to have closed 90 per cent of its gender gap (Whiting, 2023). Naturally, you might assume that this progress would mean there are higher numbers of men in primary and early year's education. Surely, in the most gender-equal country in the world, more men would feel encouraged to work with young children? Well, the reality tells a different story. Although numbers of men are higher, it's not by much. As of 2022, men make up only 18 per cent of Iceland's primary teachers and just 8 per cent of the early years workforce (Dyvik, 2024a, 2024b). Why are these numbers still so low? In 2022, Jóhannesson, Ottesen and Bjarnadóttir carried out interviews with Icelandic male teachers, which revealed very familiar challenges:

- the expectation to act as natural disciplinarians;
- the feeling of being wanted solely for what are perceived to be male-specific skills; and
- the fear that working closely with children might be misunderstood.

In other words, despite its reputation for progress in gender equality, Iceland's struggles to recruit male teachers mirror those of many other countries. So what happens when there is a direct effort to improve the numbers? To investigate this, Australia provides an interesting example. In 2023, the New South Wales Department for Education reported that, despite a four-year diversity and inclusion strategy, the number of male primary teachers had not only stagnated but declined by 24 per cent (Harris, 2023). Social media campaigns, male role models at career fairs and work experience programs failed to stop the downward trend.

These examples highlight two critical points. First, while Iceland's case suggests that cultural progress alone doesn't break gendered barriers, Australia's case suggests that even targeted strategies can fail. Second, if cultural shifts don't make a difference, and direct recruitment efforts don't always work, could the problem be investment? Although Australia took steps to increase male recruitment, none of these strategies were particularly costly. Compared to the large-scale, well-funded initiatives that have driven progress for women in STEM and business, efforts to attract men into HEED roles remains relatively small. So, this brings us to a more uncomfortable question: does getting more men into HEED professions actually matter to most people?

Historically, the push for gender equality has been about fixing long-standing imbalances that overwhelmingly disadvantaged women. Women have been excluded from opportunities and paid less for the same work. To push for real change, the response to this has been well supported. But when it comes to increasing men's representation in female-dominated fields, the urgency just doesn't seem to be the same. Jeremy Davies of the Fatherhood Institute made this contrast clear when he reflected on his 2018 research into how best to market early years teaching to men (Davies, 2023): 'How was the Ministry of Defence, in 2019, able to find £2.5 million to spend on marketing careers in the military to women, while at exactly the same time the DfE could only stump up £30,000 for us?'

The difference in investment here is huge. Women's participation in male-dominated fields has been seen as an urgent priority. Men's participation in HEED professions has not. So does that mean we should give up? Not necessarily. One country has demonstrated that meaningful change is possible, but it required something different – more than just cultural progress, and more than just scattered recruitment efforts.

A RARE SUCCESS STORY

Norway offers a more optimistic example of what is possible. Ranked second globally for gender equality, the country has made big strides in diversifying its teaching workforce. While men make up just 10 per cent of early years staff, this represents a fivefold increase since the early 1990s (Dyvik, 2024c). In primary schools, 26 per cent of teachers are now men, a figure significantly higher than in most countries (Statistics Norway, 2024). So, what has Norway done differently? Quite a lot, actually:

- national action plans, including recruitment campaigns targeting men;
- legislative measures allowing positive discrimination, prioritising male candidates when qualifications are equal;
- regional initiatives, including recognition for childcare centres where at least 20 per cent of the employees are male (Nordic Information on Gender [NIKK], 2018);

Norway's approach is comprehensive and underpinned by strong government support. For instance, Norway spends the highest percentage of public income on early childhood education and care among OECD countries (Nygård, Drahus, and Boateng, 2019). This investment encourages workforce participation for mothers, reduces the gender pay gap and helps build a more gender-equitable society overall. Norway has done more than most to increase male participation in these roles. However, when the numbers are flipped, women still make up 74 per cent of the primary workforce and 90 per cent of early years; so does this suggest that gendered career patterns are simply too ingrained to shift much further? Or, as some argue, is the issue less about social barriers and more about natural differences?

WHAT SHAPES OUR CAREER CHOICES?

When trying to understand the reasons behind the low number of men in primary teaching, it's tempting to start with the simple explanation that men and women are just different. Maybe the numbers just reflect the natural differences that influence the career paths we choose and gendered job segregation is a result of these natural differences. The argument often goes: if women dominate nursing and men dominate mining, is that really a problem? Shouldn't we simply accept that these jobs align with what people naturally want to do?

One of the most well-known voices making this case is psychologist Jordan Peterson. He points to these Scandinavian countries and argues that when men and women are given maximum freedom to choose their careers, they tend to gravitate toward traditional roles. He explains that, in places like Norway, 'Men and women won't sort themselves into the same categories if you leave them alone to do it of their own accord'. In his view, these patterns are a result of fundamental biological differences, not systemic barriers, and any attempt to force equal outcomes would require 'tremendous social pressure and tyranny' (McCulloch, 2018).

This perspective is often summarised as men like things, women like people and it gathers real momentum online. And many people find this argument compelling. When an article in the *Daily Mail* (Shaheen, 2022) discussed research into why men were underrepresented in teaching and nursing, reader comments quickly reinforced this view, suggesting that it is unproblematic for men and women to like and do different things, or emphasising this was somehow biological fact and not due to societal factors, or articulating homophobic talking points about male nurses, or implying that 'normal' men would not work with children due to fears of litigation.

The last comment, in particular, touches on another powerful force at play: the social stigma surrounding men working with children, which I discuss in Chapter 10. But even beyond this, the sheer certainty with which people state that gendered career choices are natural and inevitable is worth examining. Because, if that's true, then maybe the lack of men in primary isn't about barriers at all. It's just that most men don't want to do it. But is it really that straightforward? It's a question that stayed with me as I researched this chapter and, as it turns out, one that followed me to a party.

It wasn't a formal event – just a gathering of parents and their kids. There were about ten children there, a mix of boys and girls, and, as these things often go, the adults tried to socialise, reminiscing about the days before children, while the children had other plans entirely. What struck me that evening, and perhaps I was more attuned to it because I'd been thinking a lot about gender, was how the children naturally split into two groups. The boys, slightly outnumbering the girls, were recreating something that could only be described as Wrestle Mania. They were diving over sofas, tackling each other and sliding across the wooden floors like footballers celebrating a last-minute goal. You could hear the thuds and clatters from rooms away.

Meanwhile, my own two daughters were nowhere to be seen in this chaos. I found them in another room, sitting quietly with the other girls, plaiting each other's hair. It was quite the contrast. As the evening went on, the parents began to comment on the differences. The mums of boys laughed as they shared Instagram reels about 'boy mum life', showing images of destroyed living rooms and endless fighting. I tried to convince them that I've certainly had my share of bedlam, but they didn't seem convinced it was anywhere near what they had to put up with.

This idea of boys being innately more boisterous is a familiar one. British comedian Ellie Taylor (2024) shared her own humorous take on this during a Radio 2 interview. She admitted she initially dismissed warnings about boys being wild as outdated stereotypes. However, a year into raising her son, she conceded, describing him as a 'one-man stag do'. Popular author and psychologist, Steven Pinker (2005), adds another layer to this conversation. He once joked that there's a name for people who believe boys and girls are born nearly identical and that any differences between them are purely the result of social conditioning. That name, he said, is 'childless'.

At first glance, it's hard to argue with the idea that boys and girls, on average, are just different. We see it in how they play, how they communicate and how they react to the world around them. Popular culture and self-help books often reinforce these ideas about how men and women supposedly think and behave in fundamentally different ways, for example, John Gray's famous book *Men are from Mars, Women are from Venus* (1992). They tell us that men are better at reading maps, while women excel at reading emotions. Men are said to be logical problem-solvers, while women are multitaskers. Women, some claim, struggle to park cars, while men are supposed to be great at fixing things, as long as they can focus on one task at a time.

These stereotypes, repeated often enough, can start to sound like universal truths, affecting how we view not just individuals but entire professions. For example, the idea that women are naturally more nurturing and men are naturally more authoritative has long influenced who becomes a primary school teacher and who climbs the corporate ladder. These differences have even been the source of many a sketch show skit (Harry Enfield's 'Women: Know your limits!') and material for observational stand-ups, like Al Murray's Pub Landlord, quipping, 'Pint for the fella, glass of white wine for the lady.' Audiences love it.

But what does the science really say about the way men and women think and behave? As explored earlier in this chapter, gender norms start before a child is even born. Rippon (2020) believes that 'a gendered world makes a gendered brain', arguing that children's plastic, adaptable brains are deeply influenced by the social rules and expectations that they encounter. One of the most well-known examples of this plasticity comes from London Black Taxi drivers, whose hippocampi – responsible for memory and spatial navigation – are enlarged due to the extensive knowledge required to navigate the city's complex streets. So, if the very shape of the brain can be changed through experience, it raises an important question: are the differences we see between men and women all down to biology? Of course, it would be ridiculous to deny that differences exist. But it's just as misguided to assume that all of those differences are purely biological. The real question isn't whether men and women differ, but why? How much of what we see as 'natural' is actually shaped by the world around us?

ARE BRAINS GENDERED?

The issue of whether there are biological differences between male and female brains is a fraught one and an area where political positions or prior expectations seem to have a strong influence on the interpretation of scientific data.

(Kevin Mitchell, 2016)

When it comes to the science of sex differences in the brain, the message can be very contradictory. Even within the same newspaper, research findings can be framed in entirely different ways depending on the narrative being pushed. In 2013, *The Guardian* ran a headline proclaiming, 'Male and female brains wired differently, scans reveal' (Sample, 2013). Just two years later, the same newspaper published an article entitled, 'Men are from Mars, women are from Venus? New brain study says not' (Sample, 2015). So, it's no wonder that many people remain confused about what the science actually says.

Although not much to look at, the brain is an incredible organ. Weighing about 1.4 kg – a bit more than a bag of flour – and packed with billions of neurons, it controls everything we do. But for centuries, brain research has often focused less on understanding its complexity, and more on trying to prove that men and women are wired differently – and that women are inferior. Rippon's book, *The Gendered Brain* (2019), offers a comprehensive overview of how brain research has historically been used to justify rigid gender roles and inequality. This section draws heavily on her work, exploring how early misconceptions about male and female brains emerged and how modern science is deconstructing those myths.

In the Victorian era, a time of rapid scientific progress, researchers were particularly keen to use brain science to justify societal roles. They concluded that men were naturally designed for intellectual work, while women were destined for reproduction and domesticity. This binary thinking, often referred to as *gender essentialism*, suggested that differences between male and female brains were innate and fixed. Men were seen as superior thinkers and women's roles were confined to their supposed 'essence' – nurturing and caregiving. Some viewpoints from this time sound particularly extreme. French psychologist, Gustave le Bon, declared, 'Without a doubt there exist some distinguished women, very superior to the average man but they are as exceptional as the birth of any monstrosity, as, for example, of a gorilla with two heads; consequently we may neglect them entirely' (Rippon, 2019).

But how were such bold claims proven? The methods were pretty basic, to say the least. Measurements of head dimensions, skull capacity and facial angles became the go-to tools for scientists desperate to confirm their biases. Rippon recounts that one study took more than 5,000 measurements on a single skull. And she notes, men – on average larger in size - naturally had heavier brains, which was taken as definitive proof of their intellectual superiority. Yet, even during this era of 'bad' science, the cracks began to appear. Alice Lee, a researcher at University College London, challenged the claim that cranial capacity determined intelligence. She measured the skulls of 30 female students and 35 male anatomists and found that the smallest head belonged to a male anatomist, and several other men featured at the bottom of the list (McNeil, 2019). As a result, the notion of brain size equating to intellectual capability began to conveniently disappear.

By the turn of the 20th century, rather than arguing that women were inferior, the narrative changed to claiming that women were simply different. This difference wasn't framed as a deficit but as complementary. Men were natural problem-solvers, leaders and thinkers, while women excelled as mothers and caregivers. It was a softer form of essentialism, but one that still kept the patriarchy alive and kicking. And what does more modern science say? Over the years, further research has challenged these old assumptions. For instance, Janet Shibley Hyde reviewed 46 meta-analyses on cognitive variables – such as reading comprehension, mathematics and communication – and found that 78 per cent of gender differences were small or close to zero. Hyde concluded: 'It is time to consider the costs of overinflated claims of gender differences' (2005: 590). Similarly, a further study found no significant gender differences in maths skills among children from grades 2 to 11 (Hyde et al., 2008). And Lise Eliot and her colleagues (2021) reviewed data on verbal, spatial, and emotional processing abilities, finding no consistent male/female differences. These findings suggest that while differences exist, they are far smaller than commonly believed.

Now what confuses me is that, until I read about it for this book, I didn't really know this information. Maybe that's just my ignorance, but Rippon says it's often the sensationalist headlines that grab attention while the real science gets lost underneath. She cites a UCL study that analysed 3,500 UK press articles about neuroscience between 2000 and 2010. It found that research was frequently misrepresented to push ideological agendas or generate dramatic headlines (Guest, 2019). The idea of 'male' and 'female' brains exists not because it's backed by fact, but because it fits what people already think. Increasingly, science is showing us that brains do not have 'male' or 'female' features and knowing this matters because, from the earliest stages of life, children are soaking up messages about who they're supposed to be. For example, Christia Brown, a professor of psychology at the University of Kentucky explains: 'When you only funnel one type of skill building toys to half of the population, it means that half of the population are going to be the ones developing a certain set of skills or developing a certain set of interests' (Hogenboom, 2021). That might mean giving boys Lego and giving girls dolls, pushing them towards building and designing or caregiving before they can even speak. And whether or not we do this ourselves, we know this sort of behaviour and messaging happens in society all the time.

This chapter set out to examine to what extent our gendered world causes the low number of men in primary. And by now, the answer seems very obvious. From birth, we all pick up so many clues about who is supposed to do what, and the cumulative effect is that primary teaching is still seen by many as 'women's work'. Chapter 8 now takes us back through the history of men in education to help us see how and why these ideas became so ingrained. Then in Chapter 13, we return to this question of gendered messaging to consider how schools might begin to disrupt it.

Time to Reflect 7.1

1 How much of your own career choices, hobbies or interests do you think were influenced by gendered expectations? Can you think of moments where you were encouraged (or discouraged) from pursuing something because it was considered more 'masculine' or 'feminine'?

2 Before reading this chapter, what were your assumptions about differences between men's and women's brains? Has anything challenged or changed your perspective?

REFERENCES

Allen, G. (2024). '2024 general election: How many women were elected?' House of Commons Library. Available at: https://commonslibrary.parliament.uk/2024-general-election-how-many-women-were-elected/ (accessed 18 May 2025).

Daulby, J. (2019). 'Pink and blue limit us all'. In V. Porritt & K. Featherstone (eds), *10% Braver: Inspiring Women to Lead Education* (pp. 25–35). London: Sage Publications.

Davies, J. (2023). 'Encouraging more men to work in the early years sector'. *Early Years Educator*, *23*(24), 25. https://doi.org/10.12968/eyed.2023.23.24.25

Dyvik, E. H. (2024a). 'Number of personnel in pre-primary schools in Iceland, 2021, by gender'. Statista, 4 July. Available at: www.statista.com/statistics/1265164/personnel-pre-primary-schools-iceland-gender/ (accessed 18 May 2025).

Dyvik, E. H. (2024b). 'Share of teachers in primary schools in Iceland 2000–2022, by gender'. Statista, 23 August. Available at: www.statista.com/statistics/1266812/female-teachers-primary-schools-iceland/ (accessed 18 May 2025).

Dyvik, E. H. (2024c). 'Share of teachers who are men in preschool in Norway 2014–2022'. Statista, 23 August. Available at: www.statista.com/statistics/1312671/share-male-teachers-preschool-norway/ (accessed 18 May 2025).

Eliot, L., Ahmed, A., Khan, H., & Patel, J. (2021). 'Dump the 'dimorphism': comprehensive synthesis of human brain studies reveals few male-female differences beyond size'. *Neuroscience & Biobehavioral Reviews*, *125*, 667–97. https://doi.org/10.1016/j.neubiorev.2021.02.026

Girls Who Code. (2022). 'Annual report 2022'. Available at: https://girlswhocode.com/2022report/ (accessed 18 May 2025).

Gray, J. (1992). *Men are from Mars, Women are from Venus: A practical guide for improving communication and getting what you want in your relationships.* New York, NY: HarperCollins.

Guest, K. (2019). '*The Gendered Brain* by Gina Rippon review – exposing a myth'. *The Guardian*, 2 March. Available at: www.theguardian.com/books/2019/mar/02/the-gendered-brain-by-gina-rippon-review (accessed 18 May 2025).

Harris, C. (2023). 'Push for more male teachers fails to increase numbers'. *The Sydney Morning Herald*, 16 January. Available at: https://www.smh.com.au/national/nsw/

push-for-more-male-teachers-fails-to-increase-numbers-20230109-p5cbd6.html (accessed 18 May 2025).

Hogenboom, M. (2021). 'The gender biases that shape our brains'. BBC Future, 25 May. Available at: www.bbc.com/future/article/20210524-the-gender-biases-that-shape-our-brains (accessed 18 May 2025).

Hyde, J. S. (2005). 'The gender similarities hypothesis'. *American Psychologist, 60*(6), 581–592. https://doi.org/10.1037/0003-066X.60.6.581

Hyde, J. S., Lindberg, S. M., Linn, M. C., Ellis, A. B., & Williams, C. C. (2008). 'Gender similarities characterize math performance'. *Science, 321*(5888), 494–95. https://doi.org/10.1126/science.1160364

Institution of Engineering and Technology. (2024). 'Over one million women now in STEM occupations but still account for 29% of STEM workforce' [Press release, 8 March]. Available at: www.theiet.org/media/press-releases/press-releases-2024/press-releases-2024-january-march/8-march-2024-over-one-million-women-now-in-stem-occupations-but-still-account-for-29-of-stem-workforce (accessed 18 May 2025).

Jóhannesson, I. Á., Ottesen, A. R., & Bjarnadóttir, V. S. (2022). 'Natural disciplinarians or learning from the job? The first two years of seven male teachers in Icelandic compulsory schools'. *Education Inquiry, 15*(2), 188–202. https://doi.org/10.1080/20004508.2022.2080343

Kane, E. W. (2012). *The Gender Trap: Parents and the Pitfalls of Raising Boys and Girls*. New York: New York University Press.

Leonard, J. (2021). 'What are the psychological effects of gender inequality?' *Medical News Today*, 1 July. Available at: https://www.medicalnewstoday.com/articles/psychological-effects-of-gender-inequality (accessed 18 May 2025).

McCulloch, A. (2018). 'Gender equality: "Men and women are not the same and won't be"'. *Personnel Today*, 13 March. Available at: https://www.personneltoday.com/hr/jordan-peterson-gender-pay-gap-exist/ (accessed 18 May 2025).

McDowell, J. (2023). 'If you're a male primary teacher, there's a big "why are you doing that? What is wrong with you?"' Gendered expectations of male primary teachers: the 'double bind'. *Sociology Compass, 17*(12), e13145. https://doi.org/10.1111/soc4.13145

McNeill, L. (2019). 'The statistician who debunked sexist myths about skull size and intelligence'. *Smithsonian Magazine*, 14 January. Available at: https://www.smithsonianmag.com/science-nature/alice-lee-statistician-debunked-sexist-myths-skull-size-intelligence-180971241/ (accessed 18 May 2025).

Mitchell, K. (2016). 'Sex on the brain – a tale of two studies'. Wiring the Brain, 6 January. Available at: www.wiringthebrain.com/2016/01/sex-on-brain-tale-of-two-studies.html (accessed 18 May 2025).

Nordic Information on Gender (NIKK). (2018). 'Number of men in Norwegian childcare has risen fivefold'. Available at: https://nikk.no/en/number-of-men-in-norwegian-childcare-has-risen-fivefold/ (accessed 18 May 2025).

Nygård, G., Drahus, K. M., & Boateng, S. K. (2019). 'Norway spends the most on the little ones'. Statistics Norway. Available at: www.ssb.no/en/utdanning/artikler-og-publikasjoner/norway-spends-the-most-on-the-little-ones (accessed 18 May 2025).

Pinker, S. (2005). 'The science of gender and science: Pinker vs. Spelke, a debate' Harvard University. Available at: www.edge.org/event/the-science-of-gender-and-science-pinker-vs-spelke-a-debate (accessed 18 May 2025).

Rippon, G. (2019). 'When bigger isn't always better: how history got the female brain wrong'. London: Penguin Books UK. Available at: www.penguin.co.uk/articles/2019/03/how-history-got-the-female-brain-wrong-by-gina-rippon (accessed 18 May 2025).

Rippon, G. (2020). 'A gendered world makes a gendered brain' [Video]. Ted Conferences, March. Available at: https://www.ted.com/talks/gina_rippon_a_gendered_world_makes_a_gendered_brain (accessed 18 May 2025).

Robson, D. (2019). 'The sexist myths that won't die'. BBC Future, 1 October. Available at: https://www.bbc.com/future/article/20190930-the-sexist-myths-about-gender-stereotypes-that-wont-die (accessed 18 May 2025).

Rothman, B. K. (1986). *The Tentative Pregnancy: Prenatal Diagnosis and the Future of Motherhood*. London: Viking.

Sample, I. (2013). 'Male and female brains wired differently, scans reveal'. *The Guardian*, 2 December. Available at: www.theguardian.com/science/2013/dec/02/men-women-brains-wired-differently (accessed 18 May 2025).

Sample, I. (2015). 'Men are from Mars, women are from Venus? New brain study says not'. *The Guardian*, 30 November. Available at: www.theguardian.com/science/2015/nov/30/brain-sex-men-from-mars-women-venus-not-so-says-new-study (accessed 18 May 2025).

Sanders, E., & Samuels, O. (2024). 'Lionesses: Euro 2022 has helped 129,000 more girls get into football'. BBC Sport, 3 December. Available at: www.bbc.co.uk/sport/football/articles/cn8g72eged9o (accessed 18 May 2025).

Shaheen, M. (2022). 'Gender inequality deters men from becoming teachers and nurses, study finds'. *Daily Mail*, 22 December. Available at: www.dailymail.co.uk/health/article-11566617/Gender-Inequality-Deters-men-teachers-nurses-study-finds.html (accessed 18 May 2025).

Shuster, L. A. (2024). 'Women in STEM: Perceptions vs. realities'. *SWE Magazine*, 11 October. Available at: https://swe.org/magazine/women-in-stem-perceptions-vs-realities/ (accessed 18 May 2025).

Statistics Norway. (2024). 'Teachers in primary and upper secondary school, by sex and age (M) 2015–2023' [Data set, 17 June]. Statistics Norway. Available atwww.ssb.no/en/statbank/table/12282 (accessed 18 May 2025).

Taylor, E. (2024). Interview with Zoe Ball [Instagram video]. BBC Radio 2. Available at: https://www.instagram.com/reel/DB8d8jPsr5h/ (accessed 18 May 2025).

Whiting, K. (2023). 'Gender parity: Here's what leading countries are getting right'. World Economic Forum. Available at: www.weforum.org/stories/2023/06/global-gender-gap-parity/ (accessed 18 May 2025).

Woetzel, J., Madgavkar, A., Ellingrud, K., Labaye, E., Devillard, S., Kutcher, E., Manyika, J., Dobbs, R., & Krishnan, M. (2015). 'The power of parity: How advancing women's equality can add $12 trillion to global growth'. McKinsey Global Institute. Available at: https://www.mckinsey.com/featured-insights/employment-and-growth/how-advancing-womens-equality-can-add-12-trillion-to-global-growth (accessed 18 May 2025).

World Economic Forum. (2024). 'Global Gender Gap Report 2024'. Available at: https://www.weforum.org/publications/global-gender-gap-report-2024/ (accessed 18 May 2025).

8

A BRIEF HISTORY OF MEN IN PRIMARY

In England… at the start of the nineteenth century, the first infant teachers were actually men! It was only men at that particular time who were seen as having both the moral and physical strength to teach young children in the public sphere.

(Burn and Pratt Adams, 2015, p. 8)

INTRODUCTION

Teaching children may be a female-dominated field today, but as Burn and Pratt Adams point out, it has not always been this way. This chapter takes us back to the time of the early 1800s and looks at how the social, political and economic forces of the past shaped the gender balance of the teaching workforce over the past two centuries. It doesn't aim to cover every detail, but it does aim to show how ideas like the belief that women are naturally more nurturing, that men are better placed in leadership, or that boys need male teachers to instill discipline took hold.

1800S - THE EARLY TEACHING WORKFORCE

At the turn of the 19th century, there was no national education system in Britain. Formal schooling was limited and only a small number of children received any education. Schools fell into distinct categories: elite public schools for the upper classes; grammar schools, which dated back to the Tudor era; charity schools aimed at spreading Christian teachings; and 'dame' schools, which were informal settings run by older women or retired soldiers who taught basic literacy and numeracy for small wages (Parliament of the United Kingdom n.d.).

However, the landscape began to shift with figures like Robert Owen (1771–1858), a social reformer who saw education as a means of improving society. At a time when poverty was seen by the ruling classes as a personal failing, Owen took a very different view. Appalled by the harsh conditions endured by workers and their children at his cotton mills in Manchester and New Lanark, Owen believed that the poor were actually a product of the environment they were born into and therefore needed more support (Humanists UK, n.d.). So, in 1816, he established one of Britain's first infant schools, with a philosophy for learning built on kindness rather than rote learning and harsh discipline. Owen employed men and women, believing that they were both suitable for teaching 'provided they were both kindly' (Burn and Pratt Adams, 2015: 19). Still, Owen's model of a more egalitarian workforce was more of an outlier rather than the beginning of a trend.

As the century progressed, urbanisation and industrialisation increased the demand for education. More schools were needed and new educational philosophies emerged. For example, Samuel Wilderspin (1791–1866), leader of the Infant School Movement, reinforced the belief that men were better suited to teaching due to their perceived authority and discipline. His ideas reflected the 'separate spheres' ideology of the Victorian era, which placed men in public and intellectual roles while women were confined to domestic duties (Steinbach, 2025). Wilderspin 'did not believe women possessed the spiritual and intellectual powers, or the physical strength to run infant schools' (Burn and Pratt Adams, 2015: 20).

However, not everyone agreed. During this same period, Friedrich Froebel (1782–1852), a German educator and founder of the kindergarten movement, promoted a different view. Froebel emphasised nurture and play as essential components of early childhood education, which led him to insist that women were best suited to teaching young children because he believed they had an innate ability to carry out this role. He praised women as 'the educators of the human race' and advocated for their right to work outside the home as teachers (James, 2024). His ideas were popular with middle-class women of the time, who supported increased female involvement in education (Tovey, 2020). What followed was a rapid decline in male participation in infant teaching and by the end of the 1830s, 'it all but died away' (Clark, 1985, as cited in Burn and Pratt-Adams, 2015: 21).

THE 1870 EDUCATION ACT AND THE GROWING ROLE OF WOMEN

A turning point came with the 1870 Education Act, which marked the beginning of government involvement in education. It led to a huge increase in the number of school age children attending elementary school, which rose from 26 per cent in 1871 to 70 per cent by 1911 (Bergen, 1982). In this context, elementary school was the term used in Britain during the 19th and early 20th centuries to refer to basic schooling for children, roughly equivalent to primary school today. This rapid expansion of schools created an urgent demand for teachers, leading to the recruitment of women in large numbers, particularly in infant schools, and the shift in the workforce was dramatic. In 1870, there were around 12,000 certificated teachers, with roughly half of them being women. By 1880, the number had increased to more than 31,000 and, by 1895, nearly 53,000, with women making up three-fifths of the workforce (Gillard, 2018).

Many women were hired without qualifications or formal training, as it was assumed that their natural maternal instincts would kick in and the children in their care would therefore receive an adequate education. More importantly, they were paid significantly less for doing the same job as the male teachers. Murdoch (1970, cited in Demir, 2015) highlighted the contrast: 'In 1883, for example, the School Board of London specified that salaries of female teachers should be three quarters of those for male teachers of equal qualifications and experience. In 1890, male assistant teachers had an average annual salary of 117 pounds, while women earned 88 pounds for the same work.' Pay disparities like this were not unique to education. They reflected wider societal attitudes that devalued women's labour in nearly every profession. In fact, it took until 1955 for the government to finally agree to equal pay for equal work in teaching, phased in over six years (Moench, 2020).

During the Victorian era, the schools themselves were structured along strict gender lines. Infant classes were mixed gender, but from junior school onwards, children were usually separated. Boys were prepared for traditionally masculine careers, such as manual labour and military service, while girls' education focused on domestic skills like sewing, cooking and childcare (Skelton, 2001: 14). A parliamentary report at the time described girls' education as preparing them to be 'decorative, modest, marriageable beings' (Newnham College, n.d.). And this model of segregated learning went hand-in-hand with the emerging roles of teachers themselves. Male teachers were often seen as stricter, more authoritative figures, teaching older boys and enforcing discipline at a time when corporal punishment, including caning, was commonplace (Burn and Pratt Adams, 2015).

THE 20TH CENTURY

While the Victorian period laid the foundations for a female-dominated teaching profession, the 20th century brought further social change, which continued to shape the status of teaching and the roles that women were allowed to play within it.

In the years leading up to the First World War, women made up around three-quarters of the elementary teaching workforce. This was partly because men were increasingly drawn to better-paid jobs that aligned with the growing expectation that they would be the 'breadwinners'. Primary teaching, by contrast, offered modest pay and low status, making it far less attractive to men expected to support a family. As Bergen (1982: 11) explains, teachers at the time 'would have felt acutely that they were not being adequately rewarded... when their income was increasing more slowly than that of other occupations'. Compared to the growing wages in factory work or coal mining for example, teacher salaries had barely moved.

Bergen also argues that the combination of low status and limited career options for women at that time made it almost inevitable that primary teaching would become a 'female-dominated occupation' (1982: 14). And, as more and more women entered the workforce, this really cemented the belief that teaching young children was 'women's work', which, in turn, made the job even less likely to be recognised as a 'serious' or prestigious career. In Bergen's words, this 'disparagement... contributed to the continued low status of elementary teaching, a contributing factor in the inability of elementary teaching to achieve the status of "profession"' (1982: 14).

When war broke out in 1914, schools lost thousands of male teachers almost overnight. Tropp (1957, cited in Burn and Pratt Adams, 2015: 27) said that this led to the 'virtual cessation of the recruitment of men into the profession'. As a result, the education system had to adapt quickly, leading to an even greater reliance on women in the workforce. However, despite their growing numbers, women were still not trusted to teach older boys. During the war years, boys over the age of 12 were often grouped into larger classes rather than letting them be taught by a woman (Bergen, 1982: 14).

It was around this period that another pioneer of education arrived on the scene. In 1914, Margaret McMillan opened one of the first open-air nursery schools in Deptford to support the health and education of deprived children. The demand for these settings grew rapidly, and the Rachel McMillan College (named after her late sister) was opened some years later to train nursery teachers. However, the training was strictly for women only. The reasons for this were twofold: first, this reflected the maternalist thinking of the time; and second, teaching offered one of the few socially acceptable career paths for women outside the home (Liebovich, 2014). So, while McMillan's contributions to education undoubtedly improved conditions for some of the most vulnerable children, they also reinforced the idea that young children *needed* women.

Meanwhile, outside the classroom, women were becoming more politically active. Even before the war, the suffrage movement had been gaining ground, and campaigns for pay and working rights were growing. But progress was slow and the messages women in education received were full of contradictions. On one hand, schools needed them. They had stepped in during the workforce crisis caused by the war and kept the system afloat – and they were still cheaper to employ than men. On the other hand, policies like the marriage bar, which forced women to resign once they married, sent another message entirely: your work is temporary and your proper place is in the home. In 1925, a British judge even stated: 'The duty of a married woman is primarily to look after her domestic concerns and it is impossible for her to... satisfactorily act as a teacher at the same time' (Padmanabhan, 2000). The marriage bar wasn't officially lifted until the Education Act of 1944.

But policies like this weren't just about tradition; they were also about preserving social order. And at the heart of that order was the male breadwinner model. In a society where men were expected to provide and women to support, a man whose wife worked could be seen as inadequate (Burn and Pratt Adams, 2015: 27). That belief helped justify paying male teachers more while women's teaching was framed as supplemental even though, in reality, it was the backbone of the system.

And for the women who didn't marry and continued to teach, there was another stereotype waiting: the embittered spinster, a label that quietly punished them for not fulfilling societal expectations. As the novelist and journalist, Winifred Holtby, put it in 1935, 'The unmarried woman today is surrounded by doubts cast not only upon her attractiveness or her common sense, but upon her decency, her normality, even her sanity' (Oram, 1992: 413). Either way, the message at this time was clear. Women were useful to the system, but only on its terms and never beyond the limits society had set for them.

Across the Atlantic, in the 1930s, teaching carried similarly damaging associations. Carrington (2002: 292), reflecting on Waller's 1932 observations of the US system, noted that teaching was seen as a last resort for the unemployable. As Waller put it: 'The social standing of the profession is unfortunately low, and this excludes more capable than incapable persons... only persons incapable in other lines become teachers, that teaching is a failure belt, the refuge of "unsalable men and unmarriageable women"'.

By the time of the Second World War, the education system once again faced a teacher shortage. Thousands of men were conscripted and many young women were drawn into war work. To keep schools staffed, the government had to temporarily suspend the marriage bar – another example of women's labour being called upon when needed, but only on the state's terms. In the years that followed, a baby boom created a sharp rise in demand for teachers and, for a while, this actually led to an influx of men. According to Tropp (1957, cited in Burn and Pratt Adams, 2015: 28), the number of male teachers increased by more than 50 per cent, while the number of female teachers rose by just over a fifth.

By 1967, the landmark Plowden Report, which was a comprehensive review of primary education in England, had been published. It showed that in 1965, men made up only a quarter of the primary workforce, and that 40 per cent of primary schools had no male staff at all. In infant schools, the numbers were even starker. The report applauded the '97 brave men out of a total of 33,000 teachers' (Central Advisory Council for Education, 1967: 313) working in infant departments and argued that more men were needed because 'some young children, particularly boys, may respond better to teaching from a man than from a woman... It is also clear that a staff on which there are men teachers is likely to be more stable than a staff made up exclusively of women' (1967: 324). In other words, even though the report tried to challenge gender norms, it did so through a gendered lens where men brought discipline, women brought care, and children needed both. It was a missed opportunity to reframe the conversation and rebrand teaching as a universal career choice.

The 1970s and 1980s brought visible progress in the fight for gender equality. More women entered the workforce, and primary teaching – with its longer holidays – was increasingly seen as a good career to fit around raising a family. It offered a sense of purpose for many women and a professional identity outside the home. But the numbers of men in primary teaching continued to fall. In 1970, men made up a quarter of the primary teaching workforce. By 1980, that had dropped to 22 per cent. By 1990, just 20 per cent. By the turn of the century, it was down to 16 per cent, where it has hovered ever since (UK Parliament, 2011). The rise of new industries, like technology, created alternative paths that promised more status and better salaries, and these emerging careers were typically seen as 'men's work'. Primary teaching, meanwhile, became more and more associated with women. But even as classrooms became increasingly female-dominated, leadership remained largely male. The old belief that men were more naturally suited to leadership still seemed to hold weight and, in 1992, 75 per cent of primary headteachers were still men (Burn, 2002). At the same time, another divide within the profession had become even more pronounced. In early years settings, male teachers were almost entirely absent, not just in the classroom, but in leadership too. As Burn also notes, 99 per cent of infant school head teachers were women.

By the 1990s, conversations about the problems facing boys had begun. The next chapter continues the story from here, but before we leave the past behind, it's worth ending on a line from a House of Lords debate in 1998. In one striking (and rather offensive) comment, Lord Tope pulled together many of the themes we've seen across this chapter: 'Does the Minister agree that in addition to lousy pay and career prospects, one of the main reasons that men are not attracted to primary school teaching is that primary schools are perceived to be less important and to have less status than secondary schools? Therefore, it is perceived that men who wish to be primary school teachers must therefore be unambitious, effeminate or worse' (UK Parliament, 1998). And with that, our history lesson ends.

HISTORY'S LASTING IMPACT

There's something unnervingly familiar about the history of the primary teaching workforce, and many of the issues we still see in today's headlines, as discussed in Chapter 4, have their roots here. Beliefs that we're still wrestling with now were already forming back then: that teaching young children is a woman's role; that men are needed to enforce discipline; and that women's work can be paid and valued less. Unfortunately, some of these ideas haven't faded with time.

Back in Chapter 7, I asked whether society's attitudes to gender was the real villain of the men in primary story and, deep down, most readers probably already knew the answer. McDowell (2023) said it outright: that gendered expectations might not just be a barrier, but *the* barrier. And now we've seen just how far back those expectations go. Chapter 9 picks up the story and looks at what is happening now. It considers how these old ideas still shape the recruitment of male teachers; how they influence who applies, who stays and what life in the classroom feels like for male primary teachers today. And later, in Chapter 11, we'll return to the ongoing story of women in education because none of this sits in isolation.

REFERENCES

Bergen, B. H. (1982). 'Only a schoolmaster: Gender, class, and the effort to professionalize elementary teaching in England, 1870–1910'. *History of Education Quarterly, 22*(1), 1–21. https://doi.org/10.2307/367830

Burn, E. (2002). 'Do boys need male primary teachers as positive role models?' *FORUM*, *44* (1), 34–40. https://doi.org/10.2304/forum.2002.44.1.9

Burn, E. & Pratt-Adams, S. (2015). *Men Teaching Children 3–11: Dismantling Gender Barriers*. London: Bloomsbury.

Carrington, B. (2002). 'A quintessentially feminine domain? Student teachers' constructions of primary teaching as a career'. *Educational Studies*, *28*(3), 289–305. https://doi.org/10.1080/0305569022000003735

Central Advisory Council for Education (England). (1967). 'Children and their primary schools: A report of the Central Advisory Council for Education (England)'. Her Majesty's Stationery Office. Available at: www.education-uk.org/documents/plowden/plowden1967-1.html (accessed 16 May 2025).

Demir, Ç. (2015). 'The role of women in education in Victorian England'. *Journal of Educational and Instructional Studies in the World, 5* (2), 55–59. Available at: https://www.arastirmax.com/en/publication/journal-educational-and-instructional-studies-world/5/2/55-59-role-women-education-victorian-england (accessed 16 May 2025).

Gillard, D. (2018). 'Education in the UK: A history'. Available at: https://education-uk.org/history/' (accessed 16 May 2025).

Humanists UK. (n.d.). 'Robert Owen (1771–1858) | Humanist heritage – exploring the rich history and influence of humanism in the UK'. Available at: https://heritage.humanists.uk/robert-owen/(accessed 16 May 2025).

James, C. (2024). 'A call to rewild Froebel's Kindergarten'. Froebel Trust. Available at: https://www.froebel.org.uk/news/rewild-froebels-kindergarten (accessed 16 May 2025).

Liebovich, B. (2014). 'Margaret and Rachel McMillan: Their influences on open-air nursery education and early years teacher education'. *FORUM*, *56*(3), 529–40. https://doi.org/10.15730/forum.2014.56.3.529

McDowell, J. (2023). 'If you're a male primary teacher, there's a big "why are you doing that? What is wrong with you?"' Gendered expectations of male primary teachers: The 'double bind'. *Sociology Compass*, *17*(1), e13145. https://doi.org/10.1111/soc4.13145

Moench, K. M. (2020). 'The Woman Teacher documents a feminist labor union's victory'. JSTOR Daily, 31 October. Available at: https://daily.jstor.org/the-woman-teacher-documents-a-feminist-labor-unions-victory/ (accessed 16 May 2025).

Newnham College. (n.d.). 'Women's education'. Available at: https://newn.cam.ac.uk/about/history-college/womens-education (accessed 16 May 2025).

Oram, A. (1992). 'Repressed and thwarted, or bearer of the new world? The spinster in inter-war feminist discourses'. *Women's History Review, 1* (3), 413–33. https://doi.org/10.1080/09612029200200010

Padmanabhan, L. (2000). 'When women were second-class teachers'. Availabe at: *TES Magazine*, 22 December. https://www.tes.com/magazine/archive/when-women-were-second-class-teachers (accessed 16 May 2025).

Parliament of the United Kingdom. (n.d.). 'Schooling before the 19th century'. UK Parliament. Available at: www.parliament.uk/about/living-heritage/transformingsociety/livinglearning/school/overview/before19thcentury/ (accessed 16 May 2025).

Skelton, C. (2001). *Schooling the Boys: Masculinities and Primary Education*. Buckingham: Open University Press.

Steinbach, S. (2025, 25 April). 'Victorian era. *Encyclopedia Britannica'*. Available at: www.britannica.com/event/Victorian-era (accessed 16 May 2025).

Tovey, H. (2020). 'Froebel's principles and practice today' [PDF]. Froebel Trust. Available at: https://www.froebel.org.uk/uploads/documents/FT-Froebels-principles-and-practice-today.pdf (accessed 16 May 2025).

UK Parliament. (1998). 'Primary schools: Male teachers'. Hansard, 30 November, House of Lords Debates, vol. *595*, cc1–2. Available at: https://hansard.parliament.uk/lords/1998-11-30/debates/676ac6ad-a76a-4887-b37d-055037d78322/PrimarySchoolsMaleTeachers (accessed 16 May 2025).

UK Parliament. (2011). House of Lords *Hansard*, 13 July. Written answers for 13 July 2011. Available at: https://publications.parliament.uk/pa/ld201011/ldhansrd/text/110713w0001.htm (accessed 16 May 2025).

9
SEPARATING FACT FROM FICTION

The key factor here is the extinction of men as teachers in primary schools.
As a society we've seen it as essential to promote the interests and education of
girls. Now, boys are less involved, more likely to be truants, more disruptive
and less likely to take part in extra-curricular activity.

(Neil Lyndon, as cited in BBC News, 2000a)

INTRODUCTION

For decades, the government, media commentators, parents and even school leaders
have argued that we need more men in primary teaching. And, if you take a step back,
you start to notice the same arguments keep cropping up, often rooted more in assumptions
than evidence. You could almost imagine the arguments being pitched to schools
in a cheesy advert like this:

Are your boys disengaged and disinterested?
Struggling to find a football coach for after school matches?
Are your behaviour records overflowing with red warnings?
Worried that your workforce is looking a little... too female?

Well, worry no more! Introducing the **Male Primary Teacher**™,
the all-in-one solution to your school's most pressing needs!

- Comes pre-loaded with an innate knowledge of discipline - no training required.
- Boasts coaching badges for all your sporting needs.
- Instantly engages disaffected boys just by walking into the classroom.
- Doubles as a father figure for children in need of a strong male role model.

But hurry - stocks are low. Call now before they all disappear!

As ridiculous as this sounds, there has long been a gendered script attached to male teachers, influencing not only public perception but also government recruitment strategies. From the 1990s onwards, the same justifications kept appearing. In 2000, the then-Education Secretary, Estelle Morris, saw more men as a solution to boys' academic struggles, stating that, 'Recruiting more male teachers in primary schools could help tackle the long-term underachievement of boys and help develop a culture of learning among boys at an early age' (BBC News, 2000b). By 2006, Tony Sewell, an educational consultant, argued that schools had become 'too feminine for boys' (BBC News, 2006), suggesting that education had drifted towards a softer model that disengaged boys from learning. A few years later, in order to rectify such concerns, the Training and Development Agency (2008) launched a recruitment campaign stating, 'The countdown commences to recruit tomorrow's male primary school teachers', reinforcing the need for male role models in schools. And by 2011, the same narrative continued, with Michael Gove, Education Secretary at the time, repeating similar arguments: 'More male teachers are needed, especially in primary schools, to provide children who often lack male role models at home with male authority figures who can display both strength and sensitivity' (BBC News, 2011).

THE MAIN ARGUMENTS

At the heart of these calls for more men is the belief that, in greater numbers, they can help to counteract the so-called 'feminisation of education' – because men are assumed to bring something fundamentally different to teaching that women cannot provide. The term 'feminisation of education' has been used for decades, even though it is vague and has no single agreed definition. Christine Skelton (2002) suggests that it generally refers to a combination of factors:

- an overwhelmingly female workforce in primary schools;
- a shift towards a more nurturing and female-friendly learning environment; and
- concerns that female teachers may have lower expectations of boys and softer approaches to discipline.

Tied up in these concerns are four recurring beliefs: that men are needed as role models, that they are better at discipline, that they can raise boys' attainment, and that they're especially needed when father figures are absent. For many people, these arguments sound like common sense, and they are rarely questioned. But Skelton argues that making the case for male teachers in such generic terms creates a major problem because we're never clear about what kind of masculinity we're actually asking for.

Should male teachers embody traditional masculinity to engage boys? Or should they model an alternative, softer masculinity that challenges stereotypes? As Skelton puts it, 'If the "laddishness" of boys is equated with anti-school attitudes, then presumably male teachers need to be the antithesis of such masculine constructions. But if they do not draw on hegemonic forms of masculinity – such as "having a laugh", being competitive, enjoying sport – then it is likely that boys will fail to relate to them' (2009: 39). In other words, male teachers are placed in an impossible position: they are expected to 'rescue' boys, yet there is no agreed consensus on how they are supposed to do this without reinforcing the very stereotypes schools claim to be challenging.

Although we don't see so many male-focused recruitment campaigns any more, the belief that men hold the key to fixing boys' education hasn't gone away. For example, Richard Reeves, author of *Of Boys and Men* (2022), argues we must recruit more male primary teachers to reduce the gender gap in attainment. Similarly, a recent report from the Higher Education Policy Institute asks why 'we seem to be intensely relaxed about so many boys growing up with few male teachers, often in single-parent households (where the single parent is usually a mum not a dad)' (Brooks and Hillman, 2025: 5).

So, the question is: are these instincts right? Do male teachers offer something genuinely distinctive? And if so, what is it? In the next section, I'll examine the four most common arguments made for needing more men in primary schools, and consider what each one gets right and what each one gets wrong.

MEN AS ROLE MODELS

> I was quite a disruptive, hyperactive pupil in class, and when the teachers couldn't handle me, they sent me to see Sydney Pigden… I didn't have a good relationship with my stepfather, so he was the first dominant male figure in my life who had time for me and cared for me.
>
> (Ian Wright, as quoted in Frankel, 2007)

I'm certain you've seen the clip. Back in the early 2000s, footballer Ian Wright was shocked to be reunited with his old teacher, Sydney Pigden. Immediately he removes his hat as a mark of respect for someone who believed in him when few others did. Wright becomes childlike once again, and begins to sob before reaching out for a hug. This was a man who taught Wright how to read and write and coached him to become a better footballer.

I can't remember when I first saw it, but I have watched it so many times since. During one of my school inset days, the video was shown to staff, and there genuinely wasn't a dry eye in the house. Quite simply, it shows why teachers are so important and, crucially, it shows how much of a positive impact they can have on a young person's life. I like to think we all have those teachers we remember for the difference they made in our lives and, for some, that difference can be monumental and life-changing. In Wright's own words: 'I think what was more important to me than anything was how much he actually loved being a teacher. It's amazing what a teacher can do to somebody in their life' (Gallagher, 2018). Wright's story also makes a compelling argument for why we need more men in primary schools. After all, if one great male teacher can change a child's life in such a powerful way, wouldn't more male teachers mean more success stories for children like him? Wright's relationship with Mr Pigden is proof of the profound impact a caring, supportive male role model can have.

And I'm sure there are many stories like this one. I've met plenty of male teachers who've built brilliant, lasting relationships with children who really needed someone in their corner. Stories like Wright's matter and they should never be dismissed. But if we want to make the best case for why male teachers are important, we need to go deeper. We need to be clear about what we actually mean when we talk about role models – and where that argument sometimes over-reaches. And we need to ask why the role model argument always seems to reappear whenever boys are said to be in crisis.

The media seem to think we all have short memories. Each time a new generation of boys is seen as struggling, it's treated like something entirely new, but it isn't. The so-called 'boy problem' is not a modern phenomenon. Stretching back decades, there's always been a wave of panic attached to every new generation, whether it's the Teddy Boys of the 1950s, the punks of the 1970s, 'lad culture' of the 1990s, or today's fears around online influencers and 'toxic masculinity'. The solution often comes down to recruiting men to act as role models for the disaffected youth of the moment. We hear it today and we heard it back in the Plowden report in 1967. However, the concept of the male role model is problematic for several reasons.

1 It's Ambiguous

It is a term that gets thrown around a lot but it means different things to different people. It was first used by sociologist Robert Merton in the 1950s, and although the definition has evolved since then, Jacqueline Irvine called it 'an ill-defined and imprecise term that begs for more clarity and debate' (1989: 52). In 2008, Penni Cushman investigated how New Zealand primary school principals (both male and female) understood the idea of a male role model. Most of them listed qualities like 'honesty', 'integrity' and 'respect'. Cushman found that, 'the qualities just over a half of the principals look for in a male "role model" are the same qualities that they look for in any teacher' (2008: 132). Simon Brownhill reached a similar conclusion (2014). His participants came up with an enormous list of qualities they associated with role models – far too many for any one person to live up to. And again, most of them were gender neutral. So, we are left with a vague, inconsistent definition and the realisation that no two role models are the same; yet, we keep using the term like we all agree on what it means when we don't.

2 Children Don't Always see Teachers as 'Role Models'

Even if we agree on what a role model is – let's say a 'person you respect, follow, look up to or want to be like' (Bricheno and Thornton, 2007: 385) – we still need to ask the next question: do children actually see their teachers that way? Bricheno and Thornton suggest that they don't. They cite a 1999 study by Biskup and Pfister who asked a mix of male and female German students who they saw as their role model. Not one child named a teacher. Their own research reinforced this finding. When they asked the same question, only 2.4 per cent of responses said a teacher was their role model. They found that children are far more likely to look to close relatives, including siblings, than to their teachers. So, even if we do fill primary schools with more men, it doesn't guarantee boys will view them as role models: at least not in the way policymakers seem to imagine.

3 There's more to Role Models than their Gender

When people talk about role models in the context of schools, it largely focuses on gender. Boys need men; girls need women. But this is a huge oversimplification. As I already pointed out, research shows that the key qualities we admire in role models are not gendered. For example, a boy doesn't need a male teacher to see what respect looks like. Despite this, we know from earlier headlines that government policy still tends to push the idea that boys will mostly respond to men. However, Brownhill et al. say that this is problematic, because it 'undermines the place, value and benefits of female teachers for both boys and girls' (2020: 10). Moreover, even though children tend to gravitate toward adults they identify with, that identification goes far beyond gender. Race, religion, sexuality, shared interests or experiences all create connections. When we reduce role modelling to simply being about gender, we end up making teachers one-dimensional and we lose what actually might matter to the children in front of them.

Overall, the main issue with the role model label is that it asks too much of a single person. Children rarely look to just one person for inspiration. They pick up ideas, habits and values from all over the place: from family members, to peer groups, and even celebrities, it's rarely about one person showing them the way.

MEN AS FATHER FIGURES

> I don't doubt that many of the rioters out last week have no father at home. Perhaps they come from one of the neighbourhoods where it's standard for children to have a mum and not a dad... where it's normal for young men to grow up without a male role model, looking to the streets for their father figures, filled up with rage and anger.
>
> (David Cameron, 2011)

It was the mid-2000s and I had just finished university. I'd spent a year working in the data department of a bank, which mostly involved typing customer details into Excel spreadsheets. It wasn't the most thrilling job, but it paid the bills. It was during that year that I decided to finally bite the bullet and apply for teacher training. The interview day felt intense. It started with an essay on 'What Makes a Great Teacher', followed by a presentation on a subject I felt deserved more time in the curriculum. I chose music, a topic I was passionate about. Despite my confidence, I made the mistake of referencing a statistic from *The Sun* newspaper during the presentation – a choice that visibly displeased the assessing tutor.

After that, there was a final round. A speed-dating style interview, where I faced a series of quick-fire questions from practising teachers. It was during this stage that I had an experience that still sticks with me nearly two decades later. Partway through the interview, one of the teachers looked right at me and asked, 'But you do know why we need you in primary schools, don't you?' I hesitated, unsure of what she was getting at. I mumbled something vague about wanting to make a difference. She gave me an expression that suggested I was half-right. 'Not quite,' she continued, 'It's because you're a man. We need more men in primary schools. So many of the children we teach, especially the boys, don't have fathers at home. And that's where you come in.'

Up until that moment, I tried answering the questions with what I thought were the right reasons for wanting to teach. Suddenly, I felt like I was getting it all wrong. At 22, the idea of being seen as a father figure wasn't something I had even considered, and it made me second-guess how I was presenting myself. The rest of the interview passed in a blur and, a few weeks later, I received a letter informing me that I hadn't been successful. To be clear, my failure was not solely due to that comment. I lacked the necessary experience, and my presentation likely wasn't as strong as I'd hoped. The following year, I gained more experience, prepared better and ultimately secured a place on a teacher training course. Even so, those words have always stayed with me. Not because I found them offensive, but because they suggested that, for a man, teaching is never just about teaching. In her eyes, I was stepping into something more: filling a void in children's lives. And the more I spoke to others, the more I realised that my experience wasn't a one-off.

Back when Cushman was interviewing New Zealand principals, the most common reason given for wanting more men in primary schools was to support children from single-parent families. A significant number specifically mentioned the need for a 'father figure' (2008: 130). It's exactly the same message I received in that interview room and one that still surfaces regularly. In our own survey, featured in Chapter 6, several respondents also said that one of the main reasons we needed more men was that so many children came from fatherless homes. Having male teachers, they suggested, might somehow compensate for that. Sometimes, the language is more subtle. In 2023, Nick Fletcher MP conducted a survey as part of his research into the shortage of male teachers. One of the key themes from those in favour of increasing numbers was the belief that they would have a 'particular benefit for boys without male role models at home or in their community'.

It's not hard to see where this concern comes from. The latest data from the Office for National Statistics (2023) reports that 2.7 million families are headed by lone mothers – a figure that continues to rise every few years. Wood and Brownhill (2016) say that one of the drivers of this narrative is that the traditional nuclear family is held up as the ideal. Boys growing up without a father are often assumed to be missing out, or being brought up in a lesser way compared to those with a dad at home. Back in 1996, Australian psychologist Steve Biddulph (1995, cited in Martino and Kehler, 2006) said that these absent fathers were the root cause of the social and schooling issues faced by young boys, who, he claimed, were 'much more likely to be violent, to get into trouble, to do poorly in schools, and be a member of a teenage gang in adolescence' (2006: 132). And David Cameron certainly thought this still to be true when he claimed that absent fathers were partly to blame for the UK riots back in the summer of 2011.

When these fears turn towards education, the lack of men in schools is often seen as a serious problem. On a very superficial level, the story goes something like this: many young boys are growing up in households headed by women, then walking into classrooms almost entirely staffed by women. They're surrounded by women all day, every day. And what they are missing are masculine figures of authority to guide them, set boundaries, and provide the kind of firm influence traditionally associated with fathers. I'm sure we've all heard the old *cliché*: 'Wait till your father gets home!' The idea is that boys need someone firmer to keep them in check. And you hear it in the arguments about younger boys needing men for 'rough and tumble' play, because that's what their fathers would have offered, if they were around. Male teachers, from this perspective, are needed not just to teach, but to fill an emotional and behavioural gap left by absent fathers.

And when ideas like these are voiced by Prime Ministers, MPs and high-profile commentators, they carry real weight. They become part of the public consciousness and they tend to stick. But this line of thinking is also flawed for multiple reasons.

1 Teaching Isn't Parenting

Just like the idea of role models, the concept of a being a 'father figure' is vague at best. Does it mean that male teachers are supposed to be old-fashioned, strict authority figures, dishing out discipline? Or are they meant to be a caring, comforting presence for children who need support? If you asked a hundred people what qualities they associate with a father figure, you'd end up with a huge, varied list, and most of those qualities could just as easily describe a good mother.

And even if we could agree on what a father figure actually is, expecting a male teacher to step into that role is unrealistic. Being a father and being a teacher are two fundamentally different jobs. Like parents, teachers are caring and nurturing, but they must work within clear professional boundaries for safeguarding purposes. Trying to blend the two roles asks too much of teachers and risks sending confusing messages about what their professional responsibilities should be.

2 It Can Put Unnecessary Pressure on Male Teachers

Some male teachers are proud to be a positive figure in the lives of children who may not have a father at home. Several teachers shared this view in our survey. They recognised that, for some children, they might be one of the few male role models they regularly encounter. And many saw it as an opportunity to show that men can be kind, caring, emotionally honest and reliable. As I said when discussing role models, this isn't a straightforward 'yes they are' or 'no they're not' issue. In an environment where male teachers are rare, their presence (when it is positive) can stand for something important and I'll return to this idea in more depth in Chapter 12.

But it doesn't need to be more than that. For many male teachers, especially those early in their careers, being seen as a father figure can feel like a heavy burden. Some end up trying to be someone they're not, second-guessing how they should behave, or feeling that they are constantly falling short of expectations. Instead of simply being valued for their teaching skills, they find themselves boxed into a role they didn't sign up for.

3 A Father Figure, But Only for One Year

From a practical standpoint, the idea of a teacher acting as a father figure just doesn't make sense. Most teachers are in a child's life for a single year (maybe two) minus the holidays. Of course, male teachers can stand for something important during that time. You might be lucky enough to become their 'favourite teacher', help make them a better learner and support their development in all kinds of meaningful ways. But then they move on and so do you. The cycle continues. If it's good fathers we're looking for, we want them for more than a year. The relationships that we build in classrooms can be powerful and sometimes unforgettable but they are still temporary. They can't and shouldn't be expected to be a substitute for stable parenting.

4 It Reinforces Outdated Ideas about Families

As Wood and Brownhill (2018) point out, the father figure narrative is based on an outdated view of family life. It is one where a heteronormative setup of a mother and a father is seen as the ideal. Anything else is somehow seen as second-best. But that simply doesn't reflect the reality of modern families, where two mothers, two fathers, carers, or extended relatives are just as capable of raising happy, healthy children. And when the father figure idea enters schools, it sends the harmful message that female teachers aren't enough either. It suggests they're somehow too soft, too lenient, and I guarantee that this view couldn't be further from the truth. It also unfairly heaps blame onto single mothers, ignoring the systemic barriers many face. As Ruth Talbot from Save the Children puts it, 'Single parents are doing a brilliant job despite the inequalities they face. Just imagine what they could achieve if they were treated fairly.' (Talbot, 2024)

5 It Reinforces a Gender Binary

Ultimately, the father figure belief fuels the gender binary debate. It assumes that male teachers – in their supposedly fatherly way – bring discipline, strength and rough-and-tumble play to the table, perfectly complementing the female teachers who provide nurture and emotional support. But I'm certain every teacher reading this can think of multiple colleagues who don't fit these rigid descriptions.

At the risk of sounding like a broken record, men and women can embody all of these traits. One unexpected advantage of being a parent who teaches is having the long summer holidays with my children. When they were younger, this often meant hours in the local park. I was usually the only dad around, sometimes joined by the odd gran-dad now and again, and I'd see so many mums doing all the classic rough-and-tumble play we associate with fathers, while I stood pushing the swing, sipping my coffee. As I said at the very beginning of this book: teachers bring their own skills and build connections in a multitude of ways. Gender doesn't define that.

MEN AS DISCIPLINARIANS

In the case considered here, John failed to be the disciplinarian who could control an unruly class; the effect of this was that he constructed himself as a failure... he was clearly not living up to the expectations of the school, and hence, to some extent, was not demonstrating an appropriate masculinity as far as the school was concerned. This led to his departure from teaching.

(Mills, Haase & Charlton, 2008)

Not long ago, I was watching a discussion unfold on social media about discipline in schools. What caught my attention wasn't just the topic, but the suggestion that male teachers were naturally better at managing behaviour. It was one of those threads that pulls you in because something was clearly 'kicking off' and not in the way that I expected. The male voices in the conversation weren't the ones supporting the idea. Quite the opposite. Most of them were playing it down – openly saying that behaviour management wasn't about being a man, or having a particular presence, or a certain kind of voice. It was about training, experience and consistency.

But it was the comments from some female teachers that surprised me. One simply said, 'Being a man definitely gives you an automatic advantage.' Another – a senior teacher with thirty years' experience – said she'd never had problems with respect before, but that recently, 'the lack of respect male students show for female staff is shocking'. A third pointed out that while she could certainly handle difficult pupils, she didn't have 'the power of a deep male voice'. This actually reminded me of something a colleague once told me after covering a Reception class for the first time. Wanting to make a good start, he clapped his hands and said, 'Good morning, girls and boys!' The sound of his naturally deep and loud voice was so shocking to the children that three of them burst into tears!

These are just a few examples, but they speak to a wider cultural belief that says that effective behaviour management is firm, forceful, and, more often than not, male. The image of the no-nonsense male teacher, restoring order with a deep voice and a hard stare, is one many of us recognise. He doesn't plead. He doesn't stand for excuses. He lays down the law. This version of discipline has a certain appeal in our country. You hear the following from time to time: 'Sometimes they just need to see you shout.' Or 'It never did me any harm.' It's a style of authority that's not only familiar, but often celebrated. From *Coach Carter*-style films, where discipline is instilled and respect is demanded, to reality TV like *Bad Lads' Army*, based entirely on the idea that military-style shouting can straighten out wayward young men, the message is clear: a more masculine form of discipline equals better behaviour.

And then there's football. Sir Alex Ferguson's infamous 'hairdryer treatment' is the stuff of Premier League legend. His players knew that if you stepped out of line, he would let you have it, full blast, right in your face. Many ex-players say this was a crucial part of ensuring the winning mentality was sustained. This atmosphere of fear and clear lines between power and obedience created a dynasty that current fans (like me) can only dream of these days! And when we transfer this logic into schools, the image is easy to picture: a male teacher, sleeves rolled up, a no-nonsense presence, commanding the room, sanctioning hard and clamping down on every infraction.

So when the question of discipline comes up, as it so often does, it's not surprising that some people still believe we need more men in schools to bring back control. Especially now, when the evidence suggests that British schools *do* have a behaviour problem. Beyond anecdotes, the data backs it up. A 2024 BBC News survey of 9,000 teachers revealed the following:

- '30% of all teachers said they had witnessed pupils fighting during the week they responded to the questions'.
- 'Two in five said they had witnessed aggressively violent behaviour that needed an intervention in a single week'.
- '15% of secondary teachers said they have experienced sexual harassment from a pupil when working at school' (Moss and Dunkley, 2024).

Over the past few decades, this idea that more men is a solution has been repeated by politicians and recruitment agencies alike: that male teachers, through presence or toughness, are better equipped to manage discipline. For instance, there was the 'Troops to Teachers' initiative, a government scheme which aimed to fast-track ex-service men and women into classrooms. The belief was that their authority, their command and their discipline – skills honed in military settings – would bring real benefits to the classroom (Department for Education, 2013). It was, in many ways, the 'man as discipli-narian' narrative dressed up in policy form. But the results told a different story. Within a few years of its launch, although the scheme aimed to bring 2,000 veterans into the classroom, only 28 had qualified. As Richardson (2016) reported, 'many applicants did not have the pre-requisite qualifications or could not stay the rather demanding course of becoming a teacher – despite their Army heroics.' In the end, however, while there is much to celebrate about the scheme, and I have met some exceptional ex-military prac-titioners, it ultimately underestimated what the profession really demands.

When I think back to my first year of teaching, I found behaviour management genuinely difficult. I didn't find it instinctive at all. I didn't walk in and own the room just because I was male. In fact, it wasn't until I began reading more, practising specific strategies and building a proper toolkit that I made a real breakthrough. And even now, years on, I know that if I'm relying on raising my voice, I've already lost. When I've lost control, it feels awful. It doesn't work, and more importantly, it doesn't build anything lasting. In my experience, effective discipline is all about relationships, systems, skill and supportive teams.

Some of the strongest behaviour managers I've ever worked with are small in stature, softly spoken, but incredibly consistent. They don't rely on a booming voice or a looming body. They work at it. And what some people call 'natural' presence, I believe is more likely to be the result of experience, something honed over time. If men really were naturally better at managing behaviour, then Jamie Oliver's *Dream School* should have proved it. The 2011 TV series gave teenagers with few qualifications a second chance at education. Rather than staff the school with proper teachers (the ones with actual teaching degrees), Jamie enlisted a team of celebrities, known for their expertise in subjects like politics, music and art. The staff team was packed full of men. But their male presence made no difference at all to classroom behaviour.

In fact, some of the worst behaviour management came from the most high-profile men. In one episode, drama teacher and Shakespearean actor, Simon Callow, lost his temper with the class and yelled 'Shut up'. Meanwhile, across the corridor in History, historian David Starkey became embroiled in a heated argument and ended up calling a student 'fat', right in front of everyone (O'Sullivan, 2011). Some 'teachers' fared slightly better by showing more patience and awareness but one thing was clear: being a man didn't automatically command more respect, and certainly didn't equip them to manage behaviour.

Research supports this idea. In 2008 Barbara Read carried out a UK study looking at whether male and female teachers used different disciplinary approaches, and whether these differences supported the notion that more men were needed to correct a perceived decline in behaviour. The findings revealed no significant gender differences in the use of these disciplinary styles. Both male and female teachers predominantly used a mix of approaches such as direct, assertive language. As Read put it: 'There were no perceivable gender differences as to the discourses teachers utilised, thus countering the notion that male teachers provide a stronger, more "traditional" disciplinary culture in their classrooms through their language practices' (2008: 618).

A decade later, Joanne McDowell and Revert Klattenberg carried out a cross-national investigation into the linguistic discipline strategies used by male and female primary teachers in the UK and Germany, focusing on the linguistic strategies they used to manage behaviour. Once again, they found no evidence that discipline is a gendered skill. In their words: 'Men and women have a wide range of communicative skills in their linguistic arsenal. And as competent teachers, use whichever style (both masculine and feminine) required to perform their teaching role' (2018: 28).

Overall, the argument that schools need more men for discipline is problematic for two core reasons. Firstly, it completely undervalues the capability of women in managing behaviour by perpetuating a stereotype that women are softer and more lenient, which not only diminishes their professional skills but also unfairly blames them for issues like declining behaviour or boys' subsequent underachievement. And conversely, it overstates men's natural ability to discipline, putting undue pressure on some male teachers to conform to a tougher disciplinarian role. This can lead to stress, and even negative perceptions, if these men feel they must be more authoritarian than their instincts or training suggest. It can create a false image of male teachers as inherently stricter or more effective disciplinarians, which just isn't supported by evidence.

MEN TO RAISE BOYS' ATTAINMENT

The shortage of male role models in our primary school classrooms helps explain why boys trail girls so badly in term of attainment. It is a ticking time bomb that is leading to more and more boys, especially white working class boys, feeling disengaged, out-of-place and marginalised by our education system from an early age.

(Chris McGovern, in Ellis, 2016)

For decades, the gender attainment gap in education has been a cause for concern because, across the Western world, boys have been consistently lagging behind girls in key academic outcomes. This pattern starts in the earliest years of schooling and only widens as children progress through the system (Asthana, 2010). Back in the 1990s, the Chief Inspector of Schools described it as 'one of the most disturbing problems facing the education system' (Mendick, 2013). Around the same time in the USA, the same debate was especially charged. An *Atlantic* article declared: 'It's a bad time to be a boy in America. The triumphant victory of the U.S. women's soccer team at the World Cup last summer has come to symbolise the spirit of American girls. The shooting at Columbine High last spring might be said to symbolise the spirit of American boys' (Sommers, 2000).

And even today, this issue persists. In 2021, GCSE results showed that while 33 per cent of girls' results were top grades, it was only 24 per cent for boys (BBC News, 2021). As a result, many people have looked for explanations for and solutions to this academic gender gap. And one of the most common proposals? Yes, you've guessed it again – more male teachers. So far, we've seen that the role model idea is vague, the father figure narrative puts unfair pressure on men and discipline strategies aren't defined by gender. But this is our last claim: boys will do better in school if they have male teachers. It gets thrown around so often, you'd think there must be something in it. So, do male teachers actually improve boys' attainment?

In *Boys Don't Try?* Mark Roberts (2019) tells the story of a school in the southwest of England where boys were underperforming compared to girls. However, in the English department, the gender attainment gap was much narrower. Why? Well, this department was doing things differently. They had a boys-only class taught by a male teacher. And, on the surface, that decision appeared to be working. Upon observing this class, Roberts found a highly effective learning environment full of challenge, engagement and quality outcomes. The boys remarked that they 'adored' the English teacher and that 'he knew how to get the best out of them' (Pinkett and Roberts, 2019: 126).

But when Roberts considered what he was seeing more closely, he found that the teacher's success had nothing to do with the fact that he was a man. Instead, it was his expertise – his ability to challenge, motivate and create a strong learning environment – that made the difference. There was nothing in his approach that couldn't have been replicated by a skilled female teacher. The assumption that these boys performed better simply because their teacher was male didn't hold up under scrutiny.

And this finding aligns with research going back decades. The National Educational Longitudinal Study of 1988 found that teacher gender made *no difference* to attainment for boys and girls (Ehrenberg, Goldhaber and Brewer, 1995). More recent studies have reinforced this. A 2012 study examining the impact of teacher-student gender matching across multiple OECD countries found no solid evidence that having a male teacher improves boys' academic performance (Cho, 2012). The study concluded that what really matters isn't teacher gender but how skilled a person is at their job.

When I started at an all-boys grammar school in Northern Ireland back in 1996, all the teachers were male. This had always been the norm and the teachers were a mixed bunch. Some great, some not so great. The fact that they were male didn't enhance my engagement levels or contribute to building my masculine identity. I don't remember thinking much about their gender. It was just the way it was. However, by the time I reached Year 9, times were changing. New Labour was in power, Brit Pop dominated the airwaves and my school decided it was time to do something revolutionary: recruit female teachers. The old school masters were likely turning in their graves at the thought.

One of the first female teachers to join was an English teacher, who quickly became one of the most inspiring educators I had ever encountered. She taught me how to think more deeply about literature, to care about it, and to confidently offer my own opinions. Her lessons were worth looking forward to because they went beyond mere exam techniques. She made a significant impact on my educational journey, and she was one of the main reasons I chose to study English literature at university.

What Roberts saw during his observation was simply a great teacher who revisited core knowledge, pitched lessons perfectly, fostered an environment of respect and camaraderie, made students feel at home, and generally role-modelled how to be a good person. Roberts concluded: 'These pupils were thriving. But pretty much any pupils – female, male, Black, white, middle-class, working-class – would have thrived in this environment. The effect of the individual teacher was likely making all the difference' (2019: 133).

To paraphrase Liam Neeson from the film *Taken*, '[great teachers] have a very particular set of skills'. According to Peps McCrea (2024), director of education at Steplab, 'compared to things like changing class sizes, restructuring schools, or performance-related pay… the positive effects of a good teacher are way, way, way bigger than any of those other kinds of interventions or changes you can invest in'. And Dylan Wiliam (2010: 3) argues that, 'In the classrooms of the best teachers, students learn at twice the rate they do in the classrooms of average teachers – they learn in six months what students taught by the average teachers take a year to learn.'

Beyond this, the belief that male teachers inherently connect better with boys also carries significant pedagogical implications. It suggests that teaching boys and girls requires different approaches, often leading to the adoption of debunked concepts like gender-specific learning styles. Not too long ago, I found my first personal statement from 2008, where I proudly declared that my lessons catered to visual, auditory and kinaesthetic learners and that I diligently filled out lesson plans accordingly. However, we now understand that while individuals may have preferences, the concept of distinct learning styles lacks empirical support. Moreover, there's no credible evidence linking these styles to gender differences (Department for Children, Schools and Families, 2009). Training time spent on this sort of thing is a waste of teacher time and resources that would be better spent developing pedagogical strategies that cater to the full range of needs in a classroom, regardless of gender.

Some readers may think, 'Surely everyone knows that learning styles are old hat?' I like to think so, and within the bubble of teacher social media, it's easy to believe this mindset is a thing of the past. But I promise you, it's still very much alive. Just in the past few years, I've heard colleagues make comments like, 'The boys love that book and I get such good writing out of them.' Another teacher wrote in a blog: 'I have sat through a number of well-intentioned staff INSET sessions during my many years as a teacher, where I have been told that boys and girls learn differently, that boys thrive in a competitive environment and that I should consider ways to make my subject more "boy-friendly"' (Roskilly, 2019). And if you still don't believe me, try a quick online search – something like 'how to cater for boys' learning styles in the classroom'. You'll find site after site advising on how to engage boys specifically. So, this fight continues.

Overall though, it is clear that great teaching isn't about matching genders – it's about being a skilled practitioner. And while it's reassuring to know that teacher quality is what matters most, as long as girls continue to outperform boys academically, and the number of male teachers remains stagnant, the gender-attainment link will continue to find fertile ground.

WHERE DO THESE ARGUMENTS LEAVE US TODAY?

In my own career, I rarely hear people explicitly say that my being a man is a direct benefit to the boys in my class. However, there was one instance at a PTA event where a slightly inebriated dad approached me to tell me how happy he was that his son had me as a teacher. He mentioned that his son had only ever had women teachers and was only now starting to make good progress. While he meant well, it was an uncomfortable exchange. Perhaps it was just the Guinness talking, but in his mind, being a man was the magic ingredient. In reality, it was far more about my years of teaching experience and his son's natural maturing process. But this viewpoint still lingers.

These beliefs didn't appear out of nowhere. They've been repeated so often, and for so long, that they've slipped into everyday conversations about male teachers without many questioning them. The idea that men bring something different to the classroom reduces everyone to a stereotype and fails to acknowledge individual skills. For male teachers, it creates a narrow expectation that they must inherently know how to engage boys simply because they were once boys themselves; as if they can operate on some sort of genetic autopilot, effortlessly connecting with boys. It's not just unrealistic but dismissive of the knowledge, thought and craft that goes into good teaching. And for female teachers, it's simply insulting. It implies that they are less capable of connecting with boys, which couldn't be further from the truth. To say otherwise isn't just unfair, but chips away at their professional identity. It's the same old gender norms, discussed previously, rearing their ugly head again.

And when I think about the education world that excites me, gender doesn't even come into it. I'm sometimes called a bit of an 'edu-geek', and I take that as a compliment. I love the practitioner books we've seen over the last decade – books on behaviour, assessment, the science of learning and great teaching techniques – from people like Emma Turner, Tom Sherrington, Christopher Such and Daisy Christodoulou. I love the blogs, the podcasts and the social media discussions where passionate educators share what works. Not once in any of these conversations about becoming a better teacher have I heard gender mentioned. Only a collective aim to improve teaching itself.

Ultimately, these gendered arguments for more men undermine the very essence of what it means to be an effective educator. Great teaching requires intelligence, adaptability and a deep understanding of pedagogy, not just showing up as a male or female and letting genetics take the lead. As Carrington et al. (2007: 412) found in their research on the effects of teacher gender on student learning, after interviewing hundreds of 7–8 year-olds: 'The voices of the children in our study are clear: it is the teacher's pedagogic and interpersonal skills that are vital in engaging them as learners, regardless of their gender.' This is the reality we must embrace but one that becomes lost within these myths.

Yet, it's also important to acknowledge that many male primary teachers do take pride in being seen as role models, and rightly so. It was the most common response to our survey question about why more men were needed in primary schools. If people genuinely see themselves as serving that purpose, who am I to say they're wrong? The danger is when the role model label becomes *the* definition of a male primary teacher. When it's used to justify recruitment, or as a way of fighting against complex societal issues. That's when it stops being empowering and starts becoming restrictive.

If calling on men to be role models and father figures was enough to attract them into teaching, then we wouldn't be watching the numbers continue to dwindle year after year. So, the truth is, these arguments just aren't working. And they never did.

Across the country, there are so many men who would make outstanding teachers if only they saw themselves reflected in the profession, or heard a message that spoke to their potential. Casting male teachers solely as 'role models' or 'father figures' not only limits the appeal of the job, it diminishes the wide-ranging value they could bring to classrooms. By trying to 'carve a masculine niche' into primary teaching, as McDowell puts it, we end up promoting a version of the role that reinforces 'damaging stereotypes' (2023: 2). Men have so much more to offer primary education than just representing masculinity, so the sooner we stop trying to justify their presence through outdated assumptions, the closer we'll get to building a workforce that better serves our schools.

Time to Reflect 9.1

1   Have you ever assumed that boys respond better to male teachers, or that men offer something 'extra' in the classroom?
2   How could you gently challenge colleagues if you heard them make gender-based assumptions in your school?
3   If you were helping to recruit or mentor new teachers, how would this chapter shape your input?

REFERENCES

Asthana, A. (2010). 'Britain's divided schools: A disturbing portrait of inequality'. *The Guardian*, 10 October. Available at:www.theguardian.com/education/2010/oct/10/britains-divided-school-system-report (accessed 18 May 2025).

BBC News. (2000a). 'Why girls are beating lads'. BBC News, 17 August. Available at: http://news.bbc.co.uk/1/hi/education/884309.stm (accessed 18 May 2025).

BBC News. (2000b). 'More men wanted in primary schools'. BBC News, 23 August. Available at: http://news.bbc.co.uk/1/hi/education/893313.stm (accessed 18 May 2025).

BBC News. (2006). 'Schools "too feminine for boys"'. BBC News, 13 June. Available at: http://news.bbc.co.uk/1/hi/5074794.stm (accessed 18 May 2025).

BBC News. (2011). 'Call for more male primary teachers'. BBC News, 14 June. Available at:www.bbc.co.uk/news/education-14748273 (accessed 18 May 2025).

BBC News. (2021). 'GCSE results 2021: Record passes and top grades'. BBC News, 12 August. Available at: https://www.bbc.co.uk/news/education-58174253 (accessed 22 January 2026).

Bricheno, P., & Thornton, M. (2007). 'Role model, hero or champion? Children's views concerning role models'. *Educational Research, 49* (4), 383–96. https://doi.org/10.1080/00131880701717230

Brooks, M., & Hillman, N. (2025). 'Boys will be boys: The educational underachievement of boys and young men'. Higher Education Policy Institute. Available at:www.hepi.ac.uk/wp-content/uploads/2025/03/Boys-will-be-boys-The-educational-underachievement-of-boys-and-young-men.pdf (accessed: 18 May 2025).

Brownhill, S. (2014). '"Build me a male role model!": A critical exploration of the perceived qualities/characteristics of men in the early years (0–8) in England'. *Gender and Education, 26* (3), 246–61. https://doi.org/10.1080/09540253.2014.901723

Brownhill, S., Warwick, P., Warwick, J., & Brown Hajdukova, E. (2020). 'Role model' or 'facilitator'? Exploring male teachers' and male trainees' perceptions of the term 'role model' in England. *Gender and Education, 33* (6), 645–60. https://doi.org/10.1080/095 40253.2020.1825638

Cameron, D. (2011). *PM's speech on the fightback after the riots.* GOV.UK, 15 August. Available at: www.gov.uk/government/speeches/pms-speech-on-the-fightback-after-the-riots (accessed 18 May 2025).

Carrington, B., Francis, B., Hutchings, M., Skelton, C., Read, B., & Hall, I. (2007). 'Does the gender of the teacher really matter? Seven- to eight-year-olds' accounts of their interactions with their teachers'. *Educational Studies, 33* (4), 397–413. https://doi.org/10.1080/03055690701423580

Cho, I. (2012). The effect of teacher–student gender matching: Evidence from OECD countries. *Economics of Education Review, 31* (3), 54–67. https://doi.org/10.1016/j.econedurev.2012.02.002

Cushman, P. (2008). So what exactly do you want? What principals mean when they say 'male role model'. *Gender and Education, 20* (2), 123–36. https://doi.org/10.1080/09540250701805847

Department for Children, Schools and Families. (2009). *Gender and education – Mythbusters: Addressing gender and achievement: Myths and realities* (Ref. DCSF-00599-2009). https://dera.ioe.ac.uk/id/eprint/9095/1/00599-2009BKT-EN.pdf

Department for Education. (2013, June 7). *New routes for talented ex-armed forces personnel to become teachers.* GOV.UK. Available at: https://www.gov.uk/government/news/new-routes-for-talented-ex-armed-forces-personnel-to-become-teachers (last accessed 18 May 2025).

Ehrenberg, R. G., Goldhaber, D. D., & Brewer, D. J. (1995). Do teachers' race, gender, and ethnicity matter? Evidence from the National Educational Longitudinal Study of 1988. *ILR Review, 48* (3), 547–61. https://doi.org/10.1177/001979399504800312

Ellis, M. (2016). 'Crisis in primary schools as a million children need male teachers'. *Mirror,* 5 August. Available at: https://www.mirror.co.uk/news/uk-news/crisis-primary-schools-million-children-8570421 (accessed 18 May 2025).

Fletcher, N. (2023). 'MP research shows action needed and wanted to increase male teacher numbers'. Available at: www.nickfletcher.org.uk/news/mp-research-shows-action-needed-and-wanted-increase-male-teacher-numbers (accessed 18 May 2025).

Frankel, H. (2007). 'Ian Wright on his best teacher—Mr Pigden'. Tes Magazine. Available at: www.tes.com/magazine/archive/ian-wright-his-best-teacher-mr-pigden (accessed 18 May 2025).

Gallagher, A. (2018). 'He was prouder that I played for England than he was flying over Buckingham Palace during World War II'. *The42,* 22 October. Available at: www.the42.ie/ian-wright-mr-pigden-interview-arsenal-england-sydney-pigden-teacher-pilot-world-war-ii-4297909-Oct2018/ (accessed 18 May 2025).

Irvine, J. J. (1989). 'Beyond role models: An examination of cultural influences on the pedagogical perspectives of Black teachers'. *Peabody Journal of Education*, *66*(4), 51–63. https://doi.org/10.1080/01619568909538662

Martino, W., & Kehler, M. (2006). 'Male teachers and the "boy problem": An issue of recuperative masculinity politics'. *McGill Journal of Education*, *41*(2), 113–31.

McCrea, P. (2024). 'How to create expert teachers, according to Peps Mccrea'. Steplab, 8 May. Available at: https://steplab.co/resources/how-to-create-expert-teachers-according-to-peps-mccrea/66d9c8880982810001156c0d accessed 18 May 2025).

McDowell, J. (2023). 'If you're a male primary teacher, there's a big "why are you doing that? What is wrong with you?"' Gendered expectations of male primary teachers: The 'double bind'. *Sociology Compass*, *17*(12), e13145. https://doi.org/10.1111/soc4.13145

McDowell, J., & Klattenberg, R. (2018). 'Does gender matter? A cross-national investigation of primary classroom discipline'. Gender and Education, *31*(8), 947–65. https://doi.org/10.1080/09540253.2018.1458078

Mendick, H. (2013). 'Boys' underachievement'. Gender and Education Association. Available at: www.genderandeducation.com/resources-2/the-boys-underachievement-debate/ (accessed 18 May 2025).

Mills, M., Haase, M., & Charlton, E. (2008). 'Being the "right" kind of male teacher: The disciplining of John'. *Pedagogy, Culture & Society*, *16*(1), 71–84. https://doi.org/10.1080/14681360701877792

Moss, L., & Dunkley, E. (2024). 'Pupil behaviour 'getting worse' at schools in England, say teachers'. BBC News, 28 March. Available at: www.bbc.co.uk/news/education-68674568 (accessed 18 May 2025).

Office for National Statistics. (2023). 'Families and households in the UK: 2023'. Available at: /www.ons.gov.uk/peoplepopulationandcommunity/birthsdeathsandmarriages/families/bulletins/familiesandhouseholds/2023 (accessed 18 May 2025).

O'Sullivan, K. (2011). 'Jamie's Dream School: Fat lot of good it did them'. *Mirror*, 2 March. Available at: https://www.mirror.co.uk/tv/tv-previews/jamies-dream-school-fat-lot-115973 (accessed 18 May 2025).

Pinkett, M., & Roberts, M. (2019). *Boys Don't Try? Rethinking Masculinity in Schools*. London: Routledge.

Read, B. (2008). '"The world must stop when I'm talking": Gender and power relations in primary teachers' classroom talk'. *British Journal of Sociology of Education*, *29*(6), 609–21. https://doi.org/10.1080/01425690802423288

Reeves, R. V. (2022). *Of boys and men: Why the modern male is struggling, why it matters, and what to do about it*. London: Swift Press.

Reeves, R. (2024). 'The case for helping boys and men in education'. *Journal of Policy Analysis and Management*, *43*(2), 614–22. https://doi.org/10.1002/pam.22581

Richardson, H. (2016). 'Troops to Teachers scheme fails to meet targets'. BBC News, 18 February. Available at: www.bbc.co.uk/news/education-35595424 (accessed 18 May 2025).

Roskilly, K. (2019). 'Boys don't try: Rethinking masculinity in schools'. Sandringham Research School. Available at: https://researchschool.org.uk/sandringham/news/boys-dont-try-rethinking-masculinity-in-schools (accessed 18 May 2025).

Skelton, C. (2002). 'The "feminisation of schooling" or "re-masculinising" primary education?' *International Studies in Sociology of Education*, *12*(1), 77–96. https://doi.org/10.1080/09620210200200084

Skelton, C. (2009). 'Failing to get men into primary teaching: A feminist critique'. *Journal of Education Policy*, *24*(1), 39–54. https://doi.org/10.1080/02680930802412677

Sommers, C. H. (2000). 'The war against boys'. *The Atlantic*, May. Available at: www.theatlantic.com/magazine/archive/2000/05/the-war-against-boys/304659/ (accessed 18 May 2025).

Talbot, R. (2024). 'Shining a light on the inequalities faced by single parent families'. Save the Children UK. Available at: www.savethechildren.org.uk/blogs/2024/shining-a-light-on-the-inequalities-faced-by-single-parent-families (accessed 18 May 2025).

Training and Development Agency for Schools. (2008). 'Male teachers crucial as role models' [Press release, 30 September]. Wired-GOV. Available at: www.wired-gov.net/wg/wg-news-1.nsf/lfi/165850 (accessed 18 May 2025).

Wiliam, D. (2010). 'Teacher quality: Why it matters, and how to get more of it'. Paper presented at the Spectator 'Schools Revolution' conference, March 2010, London, UK. Retrieved from https://www.dylanwiliam.org/Dylan_Wiliams_website/Papers_files/Spectator%20talk.doc

Wood, P., & Brownhill, S. (2018). '"Absent fathers", and children's social and emotional learning: An exploration of the perceptions of "positive male role models" in the primary school sector'. *Gender and Education*, *30*(2), 172–86. https://doi.org/10.1080/09540253.2016.1187264

10

THE SOCIAL STIGMA

Men taking up teaching posts in the lower primary sector, particularly in the early years, are seen, at best, as 'unusual' or 'odd' and, at worst, as potential threats to the children.

(Carrington, 2002)

INTRODUCTION

A few years ago, a family friend was looking for a piano teacher for her children. There weren't many options nearby, but she eventually found someone who was qualified, experienced and ready to start. On the surface, it seemed ideal but something was bothering her. Just before the first lesson, she asked, 'Do you think it would be safer if I sat in the room? I mean, just in case?' When asked what she was worried about, she hesitated. 'Well... isn't it a bit weird leaving them alone with a man?'

You could call this sexism and leave it there. But the truth is, it's usually more complicated. Many of the people who feel this kind of unease are thoughtful, open-minded and fiercely pro-equality in most areas of their lives. But when children are involved, this particular fear has found its way in and it's incredibly hard to shift.

And that anxiety doesn't stop there. It creates a paradox at the heart of being a man in primary. Alongside the enthusiasm from parents and school leaders who say they want more men, there can be unease about their motives: why would a man choose to work with young children? For some, a man choosing to do this career triggers suspicion. As Geri Smyth concluded in her research with male primary teachers in Scotland, 'Teaching in the primary classroom form is fraught with contradictions' (Hepburn, 2013). In other words, men in primary are trusted to teach but not always trusted to be left alone with children.

This unease fuels a lingering stigma: a subtle mistrust that still surrounds men who choose to work with young children. It's rarely voiced openly, but it continues to influence how male primary teachers are seen and remains one of the biggest barriers to both recruiting and retaining them. This chapter now explores that stigma through a series of short exhibits, showing how it plays out in society, how it affects the lives of male primary teachers and how understanding it more deeply might help us respond more effectively.

WHAT IT MEANS TO BE A MAN

When I hear the word masculinity, I think of the very stereotypical stuff that's often lampooned in media – rugged beard, chopping wood, barbecue, not talking about feelings, watching Second World War films, and going to football games.

(Exhibit A – *The Guardian*, 2020)

A huge part of the problem is tied to society's idea of what it means to be a man. Being tough. Being in control. Never crying. Never showing weakness. These are some of the unwritten rules that still define masculine identity. Back in the 1990s, sociologist Raewyn Connell called this cultural ideal 'hegemonic masculinity': a version of manhood that rewards strength, dominance and stoicism, while pushing aside other ways of being male. Building on this idea, the concept of the man box – first developed by Paul Kivel and the Oakland Men's Project – describes the set of unspoken expectations that keep men trapped in rigid gender roles. You can't be emotional. You can't be soft. You can't show vulnerability. According to the Man Box 2024 report, these beliefs still 'box men in and limit their potential' (Brancatisano, 2024). And, as psychologist Heather Stevenson puts it: 'Anything that falls outside of the man box... is not only not allowed, but will strip men of their masculinity card or reject them from the tribe' (Blum, 2021). The report found that over a third of men still feel pressure to follow these rules, with 'toughness' seen as the most valued trait.

And that's where primary teaching sits awkwardly. It's a job that absolutely requires gentleness, emotional awareness and nurture. All things the man box tries to shut down. So, when men choose this profession, they're not just stepping into a classroom, they're stepping outside the very idea of what some people still think a man should be.

The media plays its part in reinforcing these stereotypes. In *Meet the Parents*, one of the recurring jokes is that Greg Focker is a male nurse, implying there must be something 'off' about him, or at least something not quite masculine enough. In *Friends*, the episode 'The One with the Male Nanny' explores similar discomfort, with Ross struggling to accept that a man could be so sensitive and suited to such a nurturing role. And I'm not pretending I watched these scenes shaking my head – I probably laughed along. They can be funny, because they tap into cultural tensions we all recognise. But that's also the point, because these portrayals rely on, and subtly reinforce, the idea that certain jobs just don't sit right on a man. And the more they get played for laughs, the more those associations stick. That doesn't cause stigma on its own but it keeps it alive.

Of course, women have also had a long history of being ridiculed or judged for entering traditionally male roles. But research suggests that masculinity is a more fragile construct. Vandello et al. (2008: 1325) describe it as a 'precarious state requiring continual social proof and validation'. In other words, men are more vulnerable to perceived challenges to their gender identity and often adjust their behaviour accordingly. So, for some men, working in professions associated with care, like nursing or education, is simply too far outside the box. The stigma attached to these roles isn't just about the job – it's about what the job says about the man doing them. As McGrath et al. put it, 'the plight of the male teacher has become one in which their masculinity is policed, questioned and scrutinised. For example, men who teach young children are frequently marginalised, and may be automatically viewed as effeminate or labelled "gay" – regardless of their masculinity or sexuality' (2019: 3).

It's important to note that it's not just old-fashioned ideas about masculinity that fuel the stigma. A big part of it comes from real cases of abuse. Some men have exploited positions of trust in schools, churches and community settings to commit unimaginable harm to children. These cases are rare, but the consequences are profound. Media coverage is intense, and rightly so because every child deserves to be safe. Still, these high-profile incidents have also cast long shadows over the profession, creating a climate of anxiety for many men. As Bonnett and Wade (2022) argue, male educators are often seen as 'guilty of association, because of their gender, and thus endure the consequences of crimes to which they are not associated'.

WHAT (SOME) PEOPLE THINK ABOUT MEN IN PRIMARY

> I have worked in childcare and education for over ten years. I have never felt mistrusted, questioned or had any trouble. I don't know what people are talking about when they say men feel uncomfortable in these roles.
>
> (Exhibit B – Anonymous social media commenter, 2022)

This is a quote I've seen versions of many times before, particularly in the MTP network, from male teachers who say they've never experienced suspicion and therefore do not feel like it's an issue. And to be clear – if that's genuinely their experience, I'm glad. We want teaching to feel like a profession where people feel comfortable and trusted. But the problem with this view is that it can end up dismissing the very real experiences of others because when researchers have interviewed male primary teachers about the barriers they face, social stigma almost always comes up.

Research from various countries has found that men in early years and primary often feel they are viewed as potential threats or regarded as not being 'real men'. This evidence challenges the belief that stigma does not exist and shows that, sadly, it is still widespread and can profoundly impact male teachers' professional identities and well-being. For example, Paul Sargent's study in the USA (2004: 174) found that male early years educators felt *intense* scrutiny, and had to 'tread a very thin line between behaving in ways deemed "too masculine" and "too feminine"', to avoid suspicion. This sentiment was echoed by participants of Joanne McDowell's 2023 UK study, which found that 'a common theme was the feeling amongst male teachers is that they were not viewed as a "real man" with some of the male teachers reported having a feeling of "guilty until proven innocent"' (2023: 8). And a recent Teacher Tapp poll found that 45 per cent of male primary teachers have received negative comments about their role, and 18 per cent said this had happened within the past year (Teacher Tapp, 2025).

But what does this suspicion look like beyond academic observations? One place to start is public discourse, where attitudes can be far less subtle and deeply uncomfortable to read.

> While a good friend of mine is a male infant teacher, generally I'm against this. Why? Most other positions that give easy access to children (for example, youth camps, sports coaches, and church groups) in both the US and Germany have had more than enough sexual abuse by men. It is just highly attractive for paedophiles to search job positions which grant access to children.
>
> (Exhibit C – A reader comment on Wade, 2012)

Sadly, this is one of many examples I could have used. Comment boards are full of them and the best course of action is to ignore and move on. There is no point trying to challenge these commentators because most aren't looking for debate – they're looking for reaction. But their presence still matters because they're part of the background noise that builds a culture. And when you work in a profession that is already stressful, that kind of noise can do further damage. But it's not only the trolls shouting online. Sometimes the suspicion is much closer to home.

> Today I took my DD2 to the school nursery, and on my way out I spotted DD1 in the playground and Mr **** was talking to her. I then heard him say "let's do your coat up so you're not cold shall we?" and he zipped up her coat. All of the other children running around had coats open and so I wondered why he had taken an interest in my DD particularly. Do I sound completely paranoid and irrational? I sat in the car watching the playground after that scared that he might approach her again.
>
> (Exhibit D – Anonymous Netmums commenter, 2017)

This was a male teacher doing up a child's coat. A small act of care and nothing more. And yet, to this parent, something didn't feel right. What makes the conversation thread more difficult to read is that, while many parents responded by reassuring her and questioning her bias, there were plenty who said they'd feel the same. This kind of thinking presents as concern but it carries the same quiet message as the piano teacher story: that having men around children might not be safe. That we don't quite trust them. But it's one thing for these attitudes to circulate in comment threads or 'safe spaces' for parental worries. Male teachers might never see them. However, every so often, the same thinking surfaces in public life from people in positions of real influence. And when it does, it causes big problems.

As an employer we're not, let's face it, most of us don't employ men as nannies, most of us don't. Now, you can call that sexist; I call that cautious and very sensible when you look at the stats. Your odds are stacked against you if you employ a man. We know paedophiles are attracted to working with children. I'm sorry, but they're the facts.

(Exhibit E, de Peyer, 2016)

On first glance, you might assume this quote is just another example of an online keyboard warrior. But they are, in fact, the words of Andrea Leadsom, a politician who, in 2016, was in the running to become the UK Prime Minister. She made the comment during an interview in the build-up to the Conservative Party leadership election. Unlike the preceding quotes, which are unpleasant but perhaps predictable, this one was shocking and dangerous. It's the kind of comment that makes you do a double take. Did she really just say that? Leadsom later tried to backtrack, but the damage was done. Because this wasn't a troll or an anxious parent watching from their car. This was a politician, almost in charge of the country, suggesting that some jobs simply aren't safe for men to do. And when someone in power gives that fear a platform, it does more than reinforce a stigma. It turns it into something that starts to feel like common sense.

HOW IT AFFECTS MEN IN THE JOB

A few years ago, primary teacher Ben King (n.d.) wrote about the quiet suspicion that sometimes comes with the job. 'Did you not fancy secondary?' people ask when he tells them what he does. I've lost count of the number of times I've been asked the same thing. And you can't help but wonder – what are they really saying? That primary isn't intellectually demanding enough? That I'd feel better working with older children? That it's not really a man's job? King also talked about the differences in how male teachers are treated when it comes to supervision and safeguarding. 'I don't enter the room when the girls are changing,' he said, 'but female teachers and TAs often think nothing of walking in on the boys. One teacher told me that his TA entered the room and said, "It's OK, boys. I've seen it all before!"' There's a real double standard here and it can feel incredibly uncomfortable. As King says, 'There is an assumption being made that I am a risk or am under suspicion; an assumption not made of my female colleagues.'

You see it even more plainly in early years settings, where care often includes the physical touch of comforting a child, changing clothes or helping them in the toilet. And yet, the expectations are not always the same for male and female staff. It's rare now, but not that long ago, cases like Malcolm Brown's happened. In 1995, he left his job at a Norwich *crèche* after being told he couldn't take girls to the toilet, even though delays meant some children wet themselves. The manager justified it by saying the rule 'reflected the attitudes of parents' – not to protect the child (Blackburne, 1995). That kind of policy would never be accepted today but the thinking behind it hasn't disappeared entirely. In McDowell's study, the men interviewed 'unanimously confirmed that school policies regarding physical contact with children differ for male and female teachers' (2023: 5).

King (n.d.) also shared how suspicion can follow you into your personal life. 'In pubs I've been drunkenly asked, "You enjoy hanging around with little kids, eh?" Someone else said to me, "Guy teachers always worry me. It's like vicars, isn't it? They love touching kids too".' Thankfully, comments like that are rare in my experience but I have been subject to them occasionally. Not long after I qualified, I was at a wedding. I was chatting outside with a friend (also a male primary teacher) when another guest interrupted and asked what we did for work. When he found out, he shrugged and said, 'No offence lads, but I don't think it's right for men to work with children. There's something weird about it.' We resisted the urge to argue because he could barely stand up as he fished around in his skinny chinos for a lighter, but it's one of those comments I have never forgotten.

Within schools themselves, some men feel pressure to perform a version of masculinity that doesn't quite match who they are. As McDowell (2023: 14) puts it, 'If [providing a masculine presence] is indeed the main reason that society appreciates men in teaching, it is understandable that men perform behaviours indexical of hegemonic masculinity, even if this goes against their own teaching style, preferences, and instincts, placing them in a double bind.' That idea of a double bind – more often used to describe the contradictory expectations women face – fits here too because male primary teachers are often caught between doing what the job genuinely requires and performing a version of themselves that feels safer or more acceptable. And this isn't just about how they speak or behave. For some men, it shapes the roles they take on and the paths they pursue. It partly explains why so many male teachers end up leading PE, maths or computing, or why they move into leadership early – sometimes before they're ready – because these roles, which are often viewed as more 'masculine' in nature, can offer a degree of protection from judgement.

But this creates two problems. First, it can stop men from teaching in a way that feels natural and authentic. This limits not only their job satisfaction, but also their ability to build the kinds of relationships that matter most in the classroom. And second, when men feel they have to behave a certain way to be accepted, we end up reinforcing the very gender stereotypes that having more men in primary is supposed to challenge.

WHAT MIGHT HELP?

Government policies and recruitment drives should cease relying on gender stereotypes to recruit more men… Policy makers should prioritise addressing gender-related issues, particularly the unjust suspicion towards men, in order to recognise the challenges faced and develop policies that support teachers at both local and national levels

(McDowell, 2023, p. 16)

Even if the government changed its recruitment messaging, it still wouldn't be enough. The stigma we've looked at in this chapter is deeply ingrained and it's kept alive not just by old stereotypes, but by real-world cases of abuse. And each one reignites the public's fear and suspicion. Changing that fear is not a quick fix. So perhaps the better question is: what can we do now for the men already in the job?

In interviews with male primary teachers, Vaughan Cruickshank et al. (2022) found a range of ways men responded to the unease around physical contact. Some avoided it altogether, fearing misinterpretation. Others took steps to protect themselves by keeping interactions public, asking children for consent before giving first aid or simply relying more on humour and verbal praise. However, a few, mostly more experienced, men, were relaxed about it. They said that nurturing children was simply 'part of the job' (2022: 982), and that mirroring female colleagues in this way was important. But those men had built years of trust. For newer teachers especially, the fear can be closer to the surface and, over time, that fear can affect mental health, job satisfaction and retention.

So how can we support those young men in teaching who don't yet feel as comfortable in their roles? One of the most powerful ways to do that, I believe, is through connection. Back when Matt and I were running MTP, one of the initiatives we trialled (and I wish we'd had the time to make more of it) was a male mentoring scheme. We simply paired up newer male teachers with more experienced ones. Although the purpose of meetings went beyond discussing stigma, the feedback was always very positive. Mentees spoke about the relief of having someone to speak to. And for the mentors, there was a sense of pride in being able to help someone else starting out in a career they love.

Of course, male teachers are also supported by their female colleagues every day. But when you're the only man on staff, there's often no one else who really gets what it feels like to carry those quiet worries. So those men tend to say nothing. And over time, that silence can wear them down. That's why mentoring, or any kind of meaningful connection, can make such a difference by giving men the chance to speak openly and realise they're not the only one carrying that tension.

REFERENCES

Anonymous Netmums commenter. (2017). 'Worried about male teaching assistant DD primary school' [Online forum thread]. Netmums, 1 January. Available at: www.netmums.com/coffeehouse/being-mum-794/children-4-11-years-60/1610678-worried-about-male-teaching-assistant-dd-primary-school.html (accessed 6 May 2025).

Blackburne, L. (1995). 'Nursery ban on male care ruled unfair'. *TES Magazine*, 4 August. Available at: www.tes.com/magazine/archive/nursery-ban-male-care-ruled-unfair (accessed 6 May 2025).

Blum, S. (2021). 'How the Man Box can help you understand masculinity as a prison'. Lifehacker. Available at: https://lifehacker.com/how-the-man-box-can-help-you-understand-masculinity-a-1847446196 (last accessed 6 May 2025).

Bonnett, T. H., & Wade, C. E. (2022). 'Procuring gender-situated voices of male early childhood professionals in Canada'. *International Journal of Early Childhood*, *55*(2), 187–204. https://doi.org/10.1007/s13158-022-00337-8

Brancatisano, E. (2024). 'Have you heard of the 'Man Box'? Here's why it can be harmful'. SBS News, 11 February. Available at: www.sbs.com.au/news/article/have-you-heard-of-the-man-box-heres-why-it-can-be-harmful/bsypqcs4l (accessed 6 May 2025).

Carrington, B. (2002). 'A quintessentially feminine domain? Student teachers' constructions of primary teaching as a career'. *Educational Studies*, *28*(3), 287–303. https://doi.org/10.1080/0305569022000003735

Cruickshank, V., Kerby, M., & Baguley, M. (2022). 'How do male primary teachers cope with the fear and uncertainty they experience in relation to physical contact?' *Education 3–13*, *50*(7), 979–92. https://doi.org/10.1080/03004279.2021.1929378

de Peyer, R. (2016). 'Andrea Leadsom suggests men should not be nannies because they may be paedophiles'. *Evening Standard*, 15 July. Available at: www.standard.co.uk/news/politics/andrea-leadsom-suggests-men-should-not-be-nannies-because-they-may-be-paedophiles-a3296421.html (accessed 6 May 2025).

Hepburn, H. (2013). 'Anxious times for male teachers in primary'. *TES Magazine*, 15 February. Available at: www.tes.com/magazine/archive/anxious-times-male-teachers-primary (accessed 6 May 2025).

King, B. (n.d.). 'Why are men teaching in primary viewed with suspicion?' *Teachwire*. Available at: www.teachwire.net/news/why-are-men-teaching-in-primary-viewed-with-suspicion/ (accessed 6 May 2025).

McDowell, J. (2023). 'If you're a male primary teacher, there's a big "why are you doing that? What is wrong with you?"' Gendered expectations of male primary teachers: The 'double bind'. *Sociology Compass*, *17*(12), e13145. https://doi.org/10.1111/soc4.13145

McGrath, K. F., Moosa, S., Van Bergen, P., & Bhana, D. (2019). 'The plight of the male teacher: An interdisciplinary and multileveled theoretical framework for researching a shortage of male teachers'. *The Journal of Men's Studies*, *28*(2), 149–64. https://doi.org/10.1177/1060826519873860

Sargent, P. (2004). 'Between a rock and a hard place: Men caught in the gender bind of early childhood education'. *The Journal of Men's Studies*, *12*(3), 173–92. https://doi.org/10.3149/jms.1203.173

Teacher Tapp. (2025). 'Nearly half of male primary teachers (45%) say they've received negative comments about their role – and 18% heard them as recently as this year'. Teacher Tapp, 6 February. Available at: https://x.com/teachertapp/status/1959964196717604986 (accessed 19 November 2025).

The Guardian. (2020). 'What does it mean to be a man? Guardian readers respond'. *The Guardian*, 13 November. Available at: www.theguardian.com/lifeandstyle/2020/nov/13/what-does-it-mean-to-be-a-man-reader-responses (accessed 6 May 2025).

Vandello, J. A., Bosson, J. K., Cohen, D., Burnaford, R. M., & Weaver, J. R. (2008). 'Precarious manhood'. *Journal of Personality and Social Psychology*, *95*(6), 1325–1339. https://doi.org/10.1037/a0012453

Wade, L. (2012). 'Germany attempts to recruit men into child care'. *The Society Pages*, 27 September. Available at: https://thesocietypages.org/socimages/2012/09/27/germany-attempts-to-recruit-men-into-child-care/ (accessed 6 May 2025).

11

THE ADVANTAGES OF BEING A MAN IN PRIMARY

I could produce for you a salacious moan-rant about how hard it is being a man in a female-dominated profession and how sad it is that my masculine needs (of which I have many) are not being met, but I shall not be doing that, because it is – on reflection – quite cushy to be a male primary school teacher.

(Jonny Walker, 2015)

INTRODUCTION

By the summer of 2022, the MTP network was beginning to slow down. After two years of high momentum and positivity, it felt like we were approaching a natural endpoint. We had always seen ourselves as a platform for educators – men in particular – to share their stories. And for a long time, it worked. The stories were well-received, the sense of community was strong and we felt we were doing something positive.

Our final batch of story-sharing continued to reflect the diversity of experiences among male primary teachers. John described how his working-class upbringing in the North East shaped his journey into teaching and drives his desire to make a difference for all children (Bee, 2022). Eli, a former Team GB swimmer, wrote about the resilience needed to navigate his first year as a teacher during the pandemic (Smales, 2022). And Seb reflected on the global nature of education, tracing his path from Germany to the UK, then to India and back again, before settling into a career in KS1 (Donath, 2022). Three very different journeys, but each one reinforcing the same message: that primary teaching can and should be a profession for people from all backgrounds.

At the time, Matt and I didn't realise these stories would be among the last we shared. We never had a formal conversation about calling it a day, but in hindsight, it was clear we were winding down. There were practical reasons. We were both busier and engagement on social media was declining. The appetite for feel-good stories about transformational moments and gap years leading to teaching was fading. The network had been a success, but we never wanted to outstay our welcome. However, looking back, there was something else. It wasn't just that momentum had slowed. It was becoming clear that certain parts of the story were missing and this was causing increasing tension.

Two moments made that clear. The first was the reaction to a blog we shared – a story of a male teacher's rapid rise from trainee to headship within a decade. On the surface, it was an inspiring read. But when we shared it, the response wasn't entirely what we expected. Some female educators commented that this story reflected a frustratingly familiar pattern of men being promoted too quickly, often over their more experienced female colleagues. And one comment stuck with me, pointing out that in a profession where women are the overwhelming majority, it is men who frequently find themselves fast-tracked into leadership roles.

At first, we weren't sure how to respond. This was a real teacher's story. He had worked hard. He had seized opportunities. But the criticism wasn't about him – it was about the system, and we hadn't really considered that before. A few months later, we shared our survey to gather more insights about male primary school teachers. The response was positive. People re-shared it and supported it. But one high-profile educator responded with this: 'I have completed it, but it sounds like male primary teachers are the victims... when 110% in my experience we are not at all. Not a lot of us teaching, but we seem to dominate the SLT and HT positions, which is not right at all.'

Again, we didn't really know what to say. Instead of pushing forward as if nothing had happened, we paused. Not because celebrating the joy of primary teaching didn't matter, but because our understanding of the bigger picture needed to evolve. Back in Chapter 5, I talked about the moment I realised I didn't know enough about the topic of men in primary to debate it with any real confidence. This was another wake-up call. But this wasn't just about a lack of knowledge – it was about a missing part of the conversation. In striving to highlight the challenges faced by male teachers, we had largely overlooked the advantages and privileges they might also enjoy. We hadn't considered how the scarcity of men could benefit them professionally. More than that, we hadn't considered what those advantages meant for female teachers: the opportunities they lost, the promotions they missed and the frustration they felt.

DO MEN REALLY HAVE AN ADVANTAGE?

'You should go for it – you'll have a high chance because you're a man.'
'I never stood a chance – I was up against the male teacher.'
'Male trainees get more leeway. You'll be fine.'

These are things I've heard in staffrooms and in passing conversations. I've had female colleagues tell me they've mentally given up in interviews when they've seen a male candidate. I've heard of internal promotions where women felt like they weren't really in the running because their competition was the only male teacher in the school. I'm not questioning these experiences. If anything, I don't really know how to respond when I hear them. For most male teachers, this advantage isn't something they consciously exploit. It's just the way things pan out. You apply for a job, you get it. You're encouraged into leadership, so you go for it. But when you step back, the pattern is hard to ignore. In our survey, one respondent said that, 'We have six male teachers in primary. Five of them are in leadership. Every time a male teacher starts, within a couple of years he has been promoted and is out of the classroom or moves on.'

So why does this happen? It's likely the result of two overlapping factors. First, there's the long-standing pattern, examined in Chapter 7, of men holding more senior positions across most professions. We know progress has been made for women, but the structures of power still, in most cases, favour men. And then you add in the second factor that in primary education, men are not only scarce, but also highly sought after. Governors want them. School leaders want them. Parents say they want them. Rather than cancelling each other out, these two factors combine. The gender norm already makes it easier for men to move into leadership. The scarcity effect then adds an extra push. And the result appears to be more male teachers being encouraged, mentored and pushed towards senior roles at a faster rate. When I think about the male teachers I know, most of them aren't classroom teachers anymore – they're in leadership. That's probably not a coincidence.

So does the data back this up? In *10% Braver* (Porritt and Featherstone, 2019) by the #WomenEd network, the authors dedicate the blurb on the book's back cover to some sobering statistics:

- At the time of writing, 62 per cent of teachers in secondary schools were women, but only 39 per cent of secondary head teachers were female.
- Only 7 per cent of women in education attempted to negotiate their initial salary compared to 57 per cent of their male counterparts.
- 1 in 4 teachers who quit the classroom in recent years were women aged 30–39.

But statistics only go so far. Numbers expose inequalities, but they don't always capture the lived realities behind them. That's why I wanted to hear from female educators directly – to listen, rather than assume. While researching this chapter, I tuned into a Teachers Talk Radio show entitled 'Do Women Face Inequality in Education?' (2024). Hosted by Hannah Wilson and Lucy Neuberger, the program shared a range of statistics and stories that highlighted the challenges women face. One comment stood out in particular: 'Either I'm not enough and I'm not qualified, or I can do all of that and then I'm criticised that I'm doing too much. So I feel, as a woman, I can't win – and I can't be the only one that feels like this.' Comments like this show the day-to-day exhaustion of working in a system that both depends upon women yet often complicates their progression.

WHAT DOES THE RESEARCH TELL US?

JB Smith's (2004) work into the advantages and disadvantages of male primary teachers found that, 'On the whole, the disadvantages are better articulated, understood, and documented than the advantages, which are often silenced and ignored.' With men in primary being so low in number, it's perhaps unsurprising that the conversation has centred on their struggles rather than examining how their scarcity can also provide advantages. Smith's research identified four benefits that male primary school teachers may encounter.

1 Employment Advantage

Some research suggests that male candidates may have an edge in getting a job, simply because schools want better gender balance. For example, Cushman (2006, cited in Cruickshank, 2012) found that 35 per cent of New Zealand principals admitted they would 'possibly' or 'definitely' favour a male candidate over a female – even if all other factors were equal. Interestingly, this preference was shared by both male and female principals.

2 A Fast Track to Promotion

Then there's the *'glass escalator'* effect, a term coined by Christine Williams (1992) to describe how men in female-dominated professions are propelled into leadership roles more quickly than their female colleagues. Cushman (2007) says that there is a lot of evidence which shows that men progress faster from beginning teacher to head teacher, contributing to their over-representation in leadership positions. However, it needs to be said that not all men want to climb the ladder so fast. Some male teachers report feeling pushed into leadership roles simply because they are men, with their motives questioned if they choose to remain in classroom teaching (Mills, Haase and Charlton, 2008). As discussed in Chapter 7, there's a tension here: leadership is often assumed to be the 'natural' path for men in education even though many express a desire to stay in the classroom.

3 Mentored, Noticed and Appreciated More

Being in the minority makes men stand out in schools, sometimes in ways that lead to more recognition and mentorship. Smith found that male teachers often develop strong relationships with male leaders, who see them as allies and take them under their wing. In addition, her interviews with female primary teachers frequently commented on how men received 'a great deal of kudos and gratitude from parents for providing role models for their sons' (2004: 9).

4 Pushed Into More 'Prestigious' Roles

Many male primary teachers naturally gravitate toward, or get nudged into, certain specialisms: sports, IT, upper Key Stage 2 classes. The pattern isn't hard to spot and resembles a summary of my own CV. As Smith (2004: 9) observed, 'Parents and students often regard these duties as being the most prestigious in the school.' Whether intentional or not, these specialisms can boost male teachers' status, reinforcing traditional ideas about what men are 'meant' to do in schools.

BEING PART OF THE SOLUTION

None of this means the challenges facing male teachers don't matter. As we've seen throughout this section of the book, they do. But so do the advantages. And the two are completely connected. If we want to understand the full picture of what it means to be a man in primary teaching, we also have to understand what it means to be a woman, and how these stories are bound together. Awareness of each other's struggles is part of the path to progress.

For male teachers, part of that means stepping up and doing the job properly. Leading well. Teaching well. Supporting others. And doing it with humility. As I mentioned in Chapter 9, back in the 2000s, some of the arguments for recruiting more men were about correcting the so-called 'feminisation' of teaching. However, funnily enough at the time, the most prominent figures in education were all men: Tim Brighouse (Chief Education Officer for Birmingham Local Authority), Doug McAvoy (General Secretary of the National Union of Teachers), Chris Woodhead (Chief Inspector of Ofsted) and Nigel de Gruchy (General Secretary of NASUWT). The profession may have been majority female, but the power and influence was not.

So what should men do with this awareness? They need to notice where the system might be quietly opening doors for them, and they need to advocate for colleagues who are being held back or shut out. The MTP network never set out to ignore these conversations, but we didn't give them the space they deserved. I'm glad this chapter has finally had the chance to rectify that.

Time to Reflect 11.1

1   Do you think leadership pathways are structured in ways that benefit men?
2   Have you noticed differences in how male and female teachers are perceived by parents, colleagues, or leadership?
3   Do you think schools still operate on traditional gender assumptions? (e.g., men as disciplinarians, women as pastoral leaders, leadership being seen as 'male').
4   What practical steps can leaders take to challenge biases when recruiting and promoting?

REFERENCES

Bee, J. (2022). 'We think, we become'. Men Teach Primary, 25 June. Available at: https://menteachprimary.wordpress.com/2022/06/25/we-think-we-become/ (accessed 18 May 2025).

Cruickshank, V. (2012). 'Why men choose to become primary teachers' [Conference paper]. Joint Australian Association for Research in Education and Asia-Pacific Educational Research Association Conference, Sydney, Australia, 2–6 December 2012. Available at: https://files.eric.ed.gov/fulltext/ED544531.pdf (accessed 18 May 2025).

Cushman, P. (2007). 'The male teacher shortage: A synthesis of research and worldwide strategies for addressing the shortage'. *KEDI Journal of Educational Policy*, 4(1), 79–98.

Donath, S. (2022). 'My journey (of becoming a primary school teacher) – from Germany to the U.K. to India and back again'. Men Teach Primary, 15 June. Available at: https://menteachprimary.wordpress.com/2022/06/15/my-journey-of-becoming-a-primary-school-teacher-from-germany-to-the-u-k-to-india-and-back-again/ (accessed 18 May 2025).

Mills, M., Haase, M., & Charlton, E. (2008). 'Being the "right" kind of male teacher: The disciplining of John'. *Pedagogy, Culture & Society*, 16(1), 71–84. https://doi.org/10.1080/14681360701877792

Porritt, V., & Featherstone, K. (eds). (2019). *10% braver: Inspiring Women to Lead Education*. London: SAGE Publications Ltd.

Smales, E. (2022). 'My journey to primary teaching and an NQT year in the COVID-19 pandemic'. Men Teach Primary, 2 June. Available at: https://menteachprimary.wordpress.com/2022/06/02/my-journey-to-primary-teaching-and-an-nqt-year-in-the-covid-19-pandemic/ (accessed 18 May 2025).

Smith, J. (2004). 'Male primary teachers: Disadvantaged or advantaged?' [Conference paper]. Australian Association for Research in Education Annual Conference, Melbourne, Australia, 28 November – 2 December 2004. Available at: www.aare.edu.au/data/publications/2004/smi04051.pdf (accessed 18 May 2025).

Teachers Talk Radio. (2024). 'Do women experience inequality in education?' 'The Late Show with Hannah Wilson and Lucy Neuburger', 10 September [Video]. YouTube. Available at: www.youtube.com/live/dTZIRf2rb3o (accessed 18 May 2025).

Walker, J. (2015). 'It's cushy to be a male primary school teacher'. *Schools Week*, 24 October. Available at: https://schoolsweek.co.uk/its-cushy-to-be-a-male-primary-school-teacher/ (accessed 18 May 2025).

Williams, C. L. (1992). 'The glass escalator: Hidden advantages for men in the "female" professions'. *Social Problems*, *39*(3), 253–67. https://doi.org/10.2307/3096961

PART III
THE WAY FORWARD

PART III

THE WAY FORWARD

12

THE CASE FOR MORE MALE PRIMARY TEACHERS

I really, really, really would have hoped for an approach from your end that would not state there must be more male teachers. No, there must be more teachers and there must be better teachers. There is nothing wrong with 80% of the teachers being female. After all, nature does tell us that the female gender has a more caring and nourishing touch than the male one.

(As quoted in Richards and Asli, 2024)

INTRODUCTION

As part of my research, I was listening to a *Teenagers Untangled* episode discussing male role models for boys when the presenters read out the above message from a listener. He'd taken offense at their previous discussion about the importance of male teachers. It started well enough, but by the time they reached the part about the 'nature' of women, I found myself cringing. And so did the presenters, who struggled to read it without stopping.

However, as much as I disagreed with this stereotype (which would be more at home in a 1950s homemaker's handbook), it reminded me of two tensions that sit at the heart of the debate around men in primary. Firstly, that a lot of people still think women *are* naturally better suited to working with children; and secondly, that if all the usual arguments for recruiting more men are flawed, as Chapter 9 showed, then it's not unreasonable to ask if it does actually matter that most primary teachers are women. If men aren't proven to raise boys' attainment, if they don't offer better discipline, and if the 'father figure' idea is more myth than reality, then why are we still trying to recruit more of them?

Back in Chapter 1, I made it clear that what matters most is having great teachers. Yet, at the same time, I argued that a more gender-mixed workforce matters too, not because men bring something uniquely valuable that women don't, but because their absence sends a powerful message about who we expect to work with young children. These two ideas aren't mutually exclusive. We can believe in prioritising teacher quality while also recognising that having more men in primary would be a good thing. We don't have to pick one or the other. But if we are going to push for greater gender diversity in the workforce, we need to be clearer about why.

That's what this chapter sets out to do. Because, despite all the information presented so far, through the stats, the stories, the history and the research, the jury's still out. Some people don't see a problem at all, whereas others believe we should have more men but aren't sure how to justify it. My job now is to explain, beyond reasonable doubt, why having more men in primary is something worth fighting for.

A SIMPLE ANSWER

The case for more men isn't about finding a silver bullet. It comes down to two core ideas.

1   To help children build wider, healthier ideas about gender and identity.
2   To challenge societal assumptions about who belongs in what job.

The reason these two points matter so much is because of where teachers work. Almost every child passes through school, meaning that teachers – perhaps more than any other profession – have the opportunity to shape young people's views of themselves and the world around them. Whether a child grows up in a household that reinforces traditional gender roles or one that challenges them, schools provide another environment through which they make sense of it all.

The 2019 Lifting Limits study described primary schools as 'powerful agents of change' (2019: 6). They're places where children interact with a range of adults outside their own families, which is why having diverse teams of staff matters. Children don't just learn from lessons or what their teachers say. They learn from what they see every day: who teaches them, who leads their school and how these adults behave. This isn't about overriding parental influence or pushing any kind of agenda but simply about ensuring that children see a staff team that reflects the richness of society itself. However, just saying we need more men for these reasons isn't enough. What does this actually look like in practice?

IMPACT ON CHILDREN

We know that male teachers aren't needed to 'save' boys, nor are they needed to solve specific problems in our schools. They just need to be there: teaching, supporting and interacting in ways that show children that men can be patient, nurturing and kind.

Having more men in primary means that children will experience a broader range of male identities, adding to what they already know from their families and communities. It's not about replacing those influences but expanding them and helping children to see that masculinity (like femininity) isn't one-dimensional.

This was something we saw through the MTP network. When we started out, we grouped all male teachers together – simply because we were so under-represented. But when we launched our blog and YouTube videos, something else became clear. There is no one type of male teacher. Some came to teaching after careers in law, business or sport. Others had always known they wanted to work with children. Some loved early years and storytelling; others thrived in KS2 with older children. Their motivations, journeys and teaching styles were different. And this variety really matters.

McGrath et al. (2019: 6) argue that schools should represent a broad spectrum of gender identities so that children do not see their own gender as a defining or limiting characteristic. They emphasise the importance of showcasing 'a range of masculinities, femininities, and alternative gender identities both between and within genders'. For men in teaching, this might mean demonstrating that masculinity isn't tied to author-ity or toughness but can include warmth, creativity and care. Something as small as a male teacher reading a story with 'the voices', joining in with classroom dancing, or kneeling to help a child with their shoelaces, challenges narrow ideas of what men do. For some children, these interactions may be the first time they've seen a man engage in these ways at all. And seeing a male teacher working under the leadership of a female headteacher reinforces another important message that leadership doesn't belong to just one gender.

And while male teachers will positively influence all children, there are also specific ways their presence can matter differently to girls and boys. Schools are one of the first places where children interact with adults outside of their immediate family and, for girls, having a male teacher can show them that there are different ways of being a man beyond those they may see at home. McGrath and Sinclair (2013) found that Australian sixth-form girls actually wanted more male teachers to learn how to interact with men outside of their family networks. Therefore, the presence of empathetic and approach-able male teachers can challenge old ideas that men have to be dominant or distant, and therefore influence the way girls think about relationships as they grow up.

For boys, the need for male teachers is often framed as the 'role model' argument but, as I argued in Chapter 9, it can be a problematic term, especially when it turns men into 'saviours', disciplinarians or stand-ins for absent fathers. Nonetheless, it can't be dis-missed outright. Some boys may well feel a stronger connection to a male teacher and, for those children, that relationship can be hugely important. Stories like Ian Wright's remind us that having just one adult who believes in you can change everything.

What we need to do instead, is to redefine what we mean by 'role model.' What boys don't need are men to come into schools to 'fix' them but they do need to see that there's more than one way to be a man. They need to see men who are patient, kind and emotionally aware. Men who turn up every day and listen, laugh and care. Men who build strong relationships (with children and colleagues) and treat people with fairness, warmth and respect. They need to see men who they can aspire to be. That, in itself, is powerful and that's the kind of role model that matters.

This is especially important right now because social media is doing its own kind of teaching by exposing some boys to figures who define masculinity in narrow, often harmful ways. One of the most recognisable names in this space is Andrew Tate, who promotes sexist and misogynistic views. In recent years, he has gained a considerable following among young males. Research from 2023 found that 17 per cent of boys aged 6–15 hold a positive view of Tate, rising to 23 per cent among 13–15-year-olds (Smith, 2023). However, it's equally important to recognise that the vast majority of young men do not hold these views. Most boys are not actively seeking out or aligning themselves with these influencers – but the fact that a significant minority are should not be ignored. And, in response, we need to ensure that boys are surrounded by more positive models of masculinity.

For boys, this makes the presence of male teachers important. Not because they need to stand in front of a class and declare, 'I'm here to show you that men can be different', but simply by being themselves. Just by being in the classroom teaching and caring, they can model a version of masculinity that is worth aspiring to. Matt Pinkett, author of *Boys Do Cry* (2023), says that male teachers should model positive male interactions in their daily practice. He advises them to 'compliment male colleagues openly, to talk lovingly about other people, and praise and salute male emotional vulnerability wherever and whenever possible'. These small moments can make a big difference in a child's development. But this doesn't begin and end with teachers; it's a collective responsibility. Boys need to see men stepping up across all areas of life – in families, in sports clubs, in youth work and in the media.

THE IMPACT ON SOCIETY

The significance of having more men in primary teaching goes beyond what happens in the classroom. Their increased presence has the power to challenge the idea that some jobs are 'for men' and others 'for women'. As discussed earlier, certain professions remain deeply gendered. STEM jobs are still mostly male, while HEED jobs, including primary teaching, remain dominated by women. And we know from Chapter 7 that this imbalance is partly shaped by societal expectations and the messages we absorb throughout our formative years. We know that right now hundreds of thousands of children in England attend primary schools with no male staff at all (Murkett, 2023). What message does that send? Well, for many boys, teaching will simply never register as a realistic career path, not because they're uninterested, but because they have rarely seen a man doing it. The fact is that without visible examples of men teaching children, many boys grow up never seeing this role as a possibility for themselves. This is backed up by research from Han, Borgonovi, and Guerriero, who set out to explore whether the under-representation of men in the teaching profession is discouraging boys from pursuing a career in teaching.

They found that 'the current underrepresentation of men is likely to lead students, particularly boys, to view teaching as an unattractive career option, resulting in even greater gender imbalances' (2020: 19).

My own story, however, is an example of what is possible when boys do grow up seeing a profession that feels open to them. Primary teaching was part of my life from an early age. I had family members who were teachers. I had brilliant male and female teachers growing up and I never once saw it as a gendered profession. When I trained to teach, I didn't think much about being a man in the job. I was too busy trying to find evidence to tick off the endless list of QTS standards. For me, primary teaching felt completely normal. And I'm sure many male readers will feel the same. But not everyone has that experience. For those who weren't taught by any men at primary, or haven't grown up around men in care-based roles, the job feels unfamiliar, even if they're interested in pursuing it. So, when they do consider it and take the leap into training, they can carry a sense of apprehension because it can feel like stepping into the unknown, or worse, into a space where they're not quite sure they belong.

That's why visibility matters because, without it, the few men who feel the pull towards teaching children may second-guess themselves. As Jo Warin (2017: 10) points out, 'it seems very plausible that men are attracted to a nursery that already has a good proportion of men as they are less likely to experience the vulnerabilities of being in a complete minority'. Her point speaks to the fear many men feel: that they'll be the odd one out, or that they're entering a profession where they won't quite fit. And if we don't do more to change that, the numbers will remain just as low in another decade.

The visibility argument is often summed up with the phrase 'You can't be what you can't see' because, if you don't see a version of yourself in a particular situation, it's hard to imagine yourself there. However, while researching this concept, I noticed that this phrase is almost exclusively applied to women breaking into leadership roles, STEM fields, and male-dominated industries, emphasising the need for women to see others breaking barriers so they can do the same. This makes sense because the gender gap has disproportionately affected women for generations. But the same principle applies in reverse. Boys need to see men in nurturing, child-focused roles, otherwise those jobs won't seem open to them.

When boys don't see men teaching in real life, they will naturally look elsewhere for clues about what men are 'meant' to do. And often, those representations come from places like the media, where (as we know from Chapter 10) men in care-based roles are often portrayed with suspicion or mockery; or their own family networks, where traditional gender roles may still dominate. When male teachers do appear on TV, they're not always aspirational. Think of Mr. Sugden, the belligerent PE teacher from *Kes*, or Andrew Lincoln's character in *Teachers*, marking books over pints in the pub. These portrayals may be funny, but they reinforce stereotypes rather than challenge them. When boys see only one kind of man in primary teaching (or none at all) they're left with a limited idea of what a male teacher is. More men means more reference points and this helps to break these outdated stereotypes.

And we've seen visibility make a real difference in other sectors. In Chapter 7, we looked at how the increased presence of women in fields like STEM, sport and politics has helped shift public expectations. These are still male-dominated areas, but seeing more women in them has made it easier for others to follow. The same logic applies to men in roles traditionally seen as 'women's work', and one of the clearest examples of this shift is in fatherhood. A few years ago, I was chatting with a friend when our children were still very young. We got onto the topic of how times had changed and he mentioned how astonished his grandfather had been watching him with his son. The sight of him changing nappies, making bottles and getting down on the floor to play was a complete contrast to the role his grandfather had played years before. His grandfather even admitted that he had never changed a nappy in his life but, to be fair to him, many men simply didn't do those sorts of things back when he was a young father. Statistics from the Fatherhood Institute (Burgess and Davies, 2017) highlight how much this has changed.

- In 1975, dads spent an average of just 15 minutes a day on childcare. By 2007, that had risen to two and a half hours.
- Today's fathers do roughly half the caregiving for pre-schoolers that mothers do – a big improvement from 50 years ago, when they did less than 15 per cent.

And public attitudes have also shifted massively. In 1987, nearly half of respondents to a general public survey agreed with the statement that a man's job is to earn money while a woman's role is to care for the home. By 2022, this had dropped significantly to just 9 per cent, reflecting a 39-percentage-point decline over time (Allen and Stevenson, 2023). I'm not sharing these statistics to suggest that fatherhood and primary teaching are the same. Teaching is much more than caregiving. While keeping children safe and happy is a fundamental part of the job, it's also a profession, which demands expertise in pedagogy, subject knowledge and understanding how children learn. But what these statistics do show is that attitudes about what men can and should do can shift.

Over time, expectations around fatherhood have changed. Dads are far more hands-on than a generation ago and today, being an active parent is seen as part of modern masculinity. We've seen the difference that visibility makes here. More men doing the work. More men setting new expectations for what being a dad should look like. More men holding each other to account. The same principle should apply to primary teaching. McGrath et al. (2019: 9) make the case clearly, arguing that more men in primary normalises their presence in these spaces, breaking down stigma and proving that teaching isn't a gendered profession: 'Encouraging diverse groups of men to work as school teachers may promote the acceptance of alternative masculinities while legitimising the role of men in children's lives.'

Of course, visibility alone won't fix the bigger workforce issues. It won't raise salaries or lighten the workload but it will help reframe what society sees as acceptable or expected for men. And that matters because we need to do more to dismantle the quiet suspicion some men still face when they choose to work with young children. Ultimately, the more men that are seen in these roles, the less unusual it seems and the more likely others are to follow. And if we want more men to feel comfortable stepping into primary classrooms, we need to think about what conditions we need to cultivate in order to make that happen. That's where we go next.

REFERENCES

Allen, J., & Stevenson, I. (2023). *British Social Attitudes 40: Gender Roles*. National Centre for Social Research. Available at: https://natcen.ac.uk/sites/default/files/2023-09/BSA%2040%20Gender%20roles.pdf (accessed 5 May 2025).

Burgess, A., & Davies, J. (2017). 'Cash or carry? Fathers combining work and care in the UK' (Executive Summary). Fatherhood Institute. Available at: www.nuffieldfoundation.org/wp-content/uploads/2017/12/Executive-summary-Cash-or-Carry-Fathers-combining-work-and-care-in-the-UK.pdf (last accessed 5 May 2025).

Han, S. W., Borgonovi, F., & Guerriero, S. (2020). 'Why don't more boys want to become teachers? The effect of a gendered profession on students' career expectations'. *International Journal of Educational Research*, 103, 101645. https://doi.org/10.1016/j.ijer.2020.101645

Lifting Limits. (2019). 'We can all be who we want to be: A whole school approach to challenging gender stereotypes and promoting gender equality in primary schools'. Available at: www.liftinglimits.org.uk/wp-content/uploads/2019/12/We-can-all-be-final-report-for-website.pdf (accessed 5 May 2025).

McGrath, K., & Sinclair, M. (2013). 'More male primary-school teachers? Social benefits for boys and girls'. *Gender and Education*, 25(5), 531–47. https://doi.org/10.1080/0954 0253.2013.796342

McGrath, K. F., Moosa, S., Van Bergen, P., & Bhana, D. (2019). 'The plight of the male teacher: An interdisciplinary and multileveled theoretical framework for researching a shortage of male teachers'. *The Journal of Men's Studies*, 28(2), 149–64. https://doi.org/10.1177/1060826519873860

Murkett, K. (2023). *The worrying decline of the male teacher. The Spectator*, 13 September. Available at: https://www.spectator.co.uk/article/the-worrying-decline-of-the-male-teacher/ (accessed 5 May 2025).

Pinkett, M. (2023). *Boys do Cry: Improving Boys' Mental Health and Wellbeing in Schools*. Oxford: David Fulton.

Richards, R., & Asli, S. (Hosts). (2024). 'Should all teens get therapy? Also, do boys actually need male role models?' [Audio podcast episode, 25 September]. In 'Parenting teenagers, untangled: The award-winning podcast for parents of teens and tweens'. Teenagers Untangled. Available at: www.teenagersuntangled.com/105-should-all-teens-get-therapy-also-do-boys-actually-need-male-role-models/ (accessed 5 May 2025).

Smith, M. (2023). 'One in six boys aged 6–15 have a positive view of Andrew Tate'. YouGov, 27 September. Available at: https://yougov.co.uk/society/articles/47419-one-in-six-boys-aged-6-15-have-a-positive-view-of-andrew-tate (accessed 5 May 2025).

Taylor & Francis Group. (2023). 'Boys need 'lessons in bromance' to tackle mental health crisis in schools' [Press release, 17 May]. Available at:

https://newsroom.taylorandfrancisgroup.com/boys-need-lessons-in-bromance-to-tackle-mental-health-crisis-in-schools/ (accessed 5 May 2025).

Warin, J. (2017). 'Conceptualising the value of male practitioners in early childhood education and care: gender balance or gender flexibility'. *Gender and Education*, *31*(3), 293–308. https://doi.org/10.1080/09540253.2017.1380172

13

BREAKING THE CYCLE

We're raising our girls to be perfect, and we're raising our boys to be brave.

(Reshma Saujani, founder of Girls Who Code, 2016)

INTRODUCTION

In Chapter 12, I outlined the case for more male teachers in primary schools. That was the *why*. This chapter is about *how* we might begin to move forward. And not by enacting quick, headline-grabbing strategies – like 'golden handshake' payments or male-specific PR campaigns – but by thinking seriously about the day-in-day-out conditions that we need to cultivate so that more men see themselves in this job and stay the course.

And when I talk about 'breaking the cycle', I'm not just talking about the numbers of men. In Chapter 1, I argued that the goal is not simply to recruit more men, but to attract the *right* type of men. Men who want to teach children, not those drawn in by financial incentives or outdated ideas about what male teachers are for. There is no benefit in increasing male numbers for the sake of it. Some strategies may boost recruitment in the short term, but the effects rarely last. As the Durham University investigation into graduate career choices found, 'career intentions are reportedly set for most students by the time they have chosen their subject at university. Once at university, incentives such as golden hellos, training salaries, or grants, make little difference' (Gorard and See, 2023). In other words, these payments don't fundamentally change who sees teaching as a viable career. They may help ease the financial burden for those already interested – which isn't a bad thing – but they don't do enough to attract new people into the profession or make it an option for those who hadn't previously seen themselves there. If we want a genuinely diverse teaching workforce in the future, we need to go further than temporary measures by creating schools where a wider range of people can imagine themselves belonging and thriving.

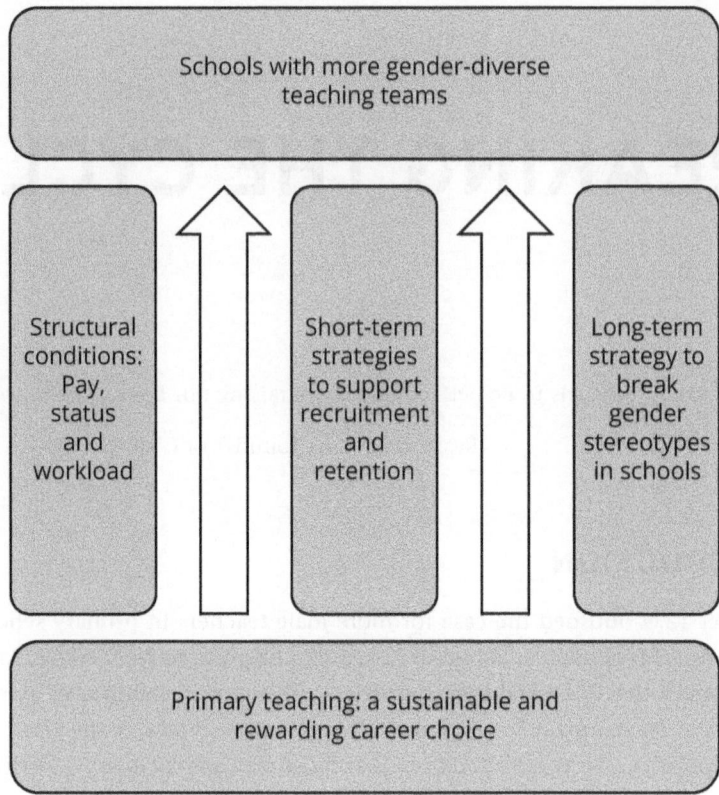

Figure 13.1 Cultivating the conditions necessary for more gender-diverse teaching teams

The above model (Figure 13.1) shows how long-term and short-term strategies must work together over time to make this goal possible. At the very base of this is the need for teaching to remain a worthwhile career, and that's why I dedicated so much of the first part of this book to celebrating how great this job can be. Without that foundation, any work to open the profession up to a wider pool of people becomes much harder because, if teaching isn't seen as a valued, sustainable career, the rest simply won't follow. Above that sits the interplay between three strands. The first is what I call the 'magic wand territory' – areas like pay, workload and conditions. These lie largely beyond our control as individual practitioners, but we still hope that those with power are listening to the profession and doing more to ensure teaching remains a career that the best students aspire to join and that great teachers want to stay in. The second strand is short-term strategies to support recruitment and retention, which I'll explore in the next chapter. But here, the focus is on the third strand: the longer-term work we can do to start shifting societal expectations about who is best suited to work with children.

When it comes to long-term change, there are two areas we need to focus on. First, we need to reflect on how deeply gendered many aspects of school life still are, from the curriculum and classroom expectations to offhand comments and the roles staff are expected to take on. Second, we need to consider the beliefs and assumptions that trainee teachers bring with them into the profession. As Jo Warin puts it, we need teachers who are 'gender-aware rather than gender blind' (2017: 26). That means helping teachers notice and challenge subtle patterns of bias and creating a culture that supports every child's identity and potential. It also means ensuring that future teachers don't feel limited by outdated expectations about what they are *supposed* to be like. This matters because if we want to open up the profession to more people – including more men – we have to start by dismantling the beliefs that keep it closed to too many.

CHALLENGING GENDERED THINKING IN OUR SCHOOLS

> My eldest son loved the colour pink as a small child but was told by strangers that he should prefer blue or purple, and once he started school, he quickly stopped saying he liked pink as he realised it is not considered a 'boys' colour.

> (Fawcett Society Report, 2020a: 37)

This section builds on the themes from Chapter 7, where I looked at how deep-rooted expectations around gender hugely influence the world children grow up in. These expectations affect everyone, but when it comes to men in primary teaching, they create a barrier that's less obvious than poor pay or challenging workloads, but no less powerful. In Chapter 12, I argued that visibility matters because when boys grow up seeing men in teaching, it helps dismantle the idea that it's a job only for women. But in reality, the current shortage of men in primary education means we cannot rely on visibility alone to shift perceptions because we simply don't have the numbers. What we can do, however, is take responsibility for the environments we create in schools. As Han, Borgonovi and Guerriero (2020: 4) argue, 'the socialisation of boys' occupational preferences... is underpinned by a culture's gender ideology'. In other words, boys are growing up in a world where certain jobs appear 'off-limits' because of how they've been gendered over time.

Schools can't change the entire labour market but they can become spaces where those gendered assumptions are actively challenged, rather than quietly reinforced. Most schools aren't ignoring this issue and, in my experience, they are trying. But the question is: are we doing enough? Do we fully understand the long-term effects that gender stereotypes have on children's sense of identity and belonging? Do we really know how to spot and challenge the subtle gender stereotypes that show up in everyday school life in what we teach, how we speak and in how we interact in front of the children? I'd argue that we're not there yet. Schools need more support and clarity to do this well because doing nothing means too many children grow up limited by outdated thinking and, in the educational world, we will continue to lose out on whole groups of men who might have made great teachers.

WHAT IMPACT DO GENDER STEREOTYPES HAVE ON CHILDREN?

From the earliest years of life, children are bombarded with messages about what is deemed acceptable for boys and girls. Some messages are plain to see, such as pink and blue gender reveals, but others are more subtly woven into toys, clothes, books and even the language adults use around them. I'm sure we've all seen this rigid gender binary in action, in shops with their princess girls' sections and superhero messaging in the boys' areas. And this sort of stereotyping doesn't stop with children. Last year, my friend sent me a photo of the Father's Day book section in his supermarket, predictably filled with action and war titles, as though men's interests must fit neatly into such narrow categories.

But these expectations go far beyond the books and toys we should desire. They send quiet but powerful signals about who gets to express which emotions, pursue which interests or imagine which futures. Comedian and writer Robert Webb has spoken openly about how these pressures affected him as he was growing up. Reflecting on his memoir *How Not to Be a Boy*, he said, 'I was acutely aware that I was shy... I thought boys were supposed to be boisterous, cheeky and cajoling' (Webb, 2017). In another interview, he said he would tell boys, 'It's OK to cry. It's OK to prefer the company of your mother, and not be that interested in sports, and to have female friends' (Beckerman, 2018). For Webb, society's rigid ideas of masculinity limited his emotional expression and caused ongoing feelings of isolation and not being true to himself. And while his story is personal, the social pressures he describes are experienced by many. Research shows that gendered beliefs begin shaping children's self-image and behaviour from a very early age.

The Fawcett Society's Commission on Gender Stereotypes in Early Childhood (2020a: 6–7) reported on some of the most significant long-term effects:

- By the age of six, girls start avoiding certain subjects because they believe they are not 'smart' enough, leading to lower participation in STEM fields later in life.
- Gender expectations cause boys' reading skills to suffer from a young age compared to girls, one of the main causes of the gender attainment gap.
- 36 per cent of 7–10-year-old girls are made to believe their physical appearance matters most, leading to body image issues and mental health crises like eating disorders.
- Narrow ideas of masculinity stop men from seeking help, contributing to high male suicide rates.

And these stereotypes don't just shape how children feel. They also influence what adults imagine their children can become. A separate summary from the Fawcett Society (2020b) revealed that parents were seven times more likely to picture their sons in construction roles than their daughters (22 per cent compared to just 3 per cent), and almost three times more likely to see their daughters in nursing or care work than their sons (22 per cent versus 8 per cent). These assumptions aren't necessarily conscious and certainly not malicious, but they are deeply rooted and they carry real weight in shaping children's sense of possibility.

Of course, schools cannot change what a child hears at home, but they can create the conditions through which those assumptions are disrupted, not reinforced. And that begins with teachers. However, the Fawcett Society report (2020b: 8) also highlighted how schools often unintentionally uphold gendered norms. For example:

- Teachers holding gender-stereotypical attitudes have been found to influence children's subject interests and success.
- Boys are more likely to receive attention in class than girls.
- Children are often praised when their actions match traditional gender expectations – girls for being helpful, boys for being active.

In the early years, more than half of practitioners surveyed had heard the phrase 'boys will be boys' used to excuse misbehaviour. Nearly half reported adults using gendered pet names like 'sweetheart' or 'buddy', and a third had seen children being split into boys-versus-girls groups for activities. Sixty per cent said that assumptions that boys and girls naturally want to do different things were common. In isolation, these may sound like small things but, over time, they're the kind of small things that 'dictate what is acceptable or expected for women and girls, and men and boys' (Fawcett Society, 2020b: 6).

In my own working life, I've experienced these dynamics. Boys are often the default choice when furniture needs moving whereas girls are asked to tidy the book corner. Once, after I had asked two girls to carry a desk, a colleague looked at me as though I'd broken some unwritten rule. And in addition to practitioners reinforcing gendered expectations, stereotyping turns up frequently in the stories we share with the children. A recent study in the US analysed 247 books for children under five and found that female protagonists were more likely to be associated with communication and domesticity, while boys were linked to careers and maths. Overall, they found that gender stereotypes were much more common in children's books than adults. As researcher Molly Lewis put it, children's books 'may be a vehicle for communicating information about gender' (Phys.org, 2021). But most educators are never made aware of just how powerful these early messages can be.

Sometimes the stereotyping is much more obvious. In 2022, a well-known head teacher stated publicly that girls were avoiding physics because, in her words, 'physics isn't something girls tend to fancy. They don't want to do it. They don't like it' (Devlin and Allegretti, 2022). The backlash was swift. Dr Jess Wade, a physicist at Imperial College London, called the remarks 'patronising, infuriating, and closing doors to exciting careers in physics and engineering for generations of young women'. She added that 'there is absolutely no evidence to show intrinsic differences in their abilities or preference'.

And she is right, but the statistics show the consequences of this sort of gendered thinking. Only 39 per cent of A-level maths students are female; for double maths, it drops to 29 per cent, and for physics, just 23 per cent (Yates, 2022).

Unfortunately, these types of views are still widespread in education. Research from large-scale assessments shows that both male and female teachers tend to rate boys as more capable in maths and girls as naturally stronger in reading (Hares, Nagesh and Konate, 2022). And these beliefs can manifest within classroom interactions. As documented in Rycroft-Smith and Andre's *The Equal Classroom* (2019: 6), 'teachers routinely choose boys to answer questions more often, allow them to speak longer and praise them differently than they praise girls'.

Becky Francis, co-chair of the Commission on Gender Stereotypes in Early Childhood, put it clearly: 'What every parent hopes for their child, and what educators hope for children in their class, is that they will be free to achieve their potential – yet what the evidence shows is that we still limit our children based on harmful, tired gender stereotypes' (Fawcett Society, 2020a: 23). Whether we like it or not, our schools are still influenced by gendered expectations and while some of the examples shared might still feel harmless or simply 'the way things are,' the long-term effects are not.

Schools can't undo every harmful message children hear outside the gates but they can take responsibility for the messages they send inside them. And, to be clear, the long-term aim is not about achieving 50:50 splits in science or care-giving roles but creating schools where children feel genuinely free to be themselves and, in the context of this book, where boys grow up seeing primary teaching as something they could do. Because unless we challenge these limits, we will keep reproducing the same barriers that stop many men from even considering the profession in the first place.

WHERE TO BEGIN?

The purpose of this chapter hasn't been to offer a checklist of strategies but to show why this work matters and what's at stake if we ignore it. Fortunately, we don't need to start from scratch because a growing number of experts have already done the heavy lifting when it comes to practical guidance. Here are three standout resources I'd recommend to any school ready to begin, revisit or deepen this work.

1 The Fawcett Society's 'Unlimited Potential' Report (2020)

This report has supported much of the thinking in this chapter. Alongside its findings, it offers clear and practical tips for teachers and school leaders who want to tackle gender stereotyping. These range from 'praising children equally, to choosing language more carefully, to having open conversations that help children form a more equal worldview' (Fawcett Society, 2020a 9). The aim is to ensure all educators (and those training to become them) are equipped to notice and challenge gender bias in their everyday practice.

2 Lifting Limits: A Whole-School Approach to Gender Equality

This is a comprehensive programme created to help primary schools identify and challenge gender stereotypes embedded in everyday school life. It begins with staff-wide training and a gender audit, followed by the appointment of a 'Gender Champion' to lead ongoing efforts. Schools are guided through the process, with resources all aimed at developing gender awareness. An independent evaluation of their pilot programme in five London primary schools demonstrated significant positive impacts on both staff practices and pupil attitudes.

3 *The Equal Classroom*, 2019

This book, edited by Louise Rycroft-Smith and Graham Andre, is a great place to start for readers seeking to develop their understanding further. While not every chapter directly addresses primary teaching, it covers a range of topics aimed at helping teachers think more carefully about how gender shows up in everyday life. Graham Andre's name might ring a bell from the 2017 BBC documentary *No More Boys and Girls*, where he worked on exploring the impact of gender expectations in his own classroom, a project that remains relevant nearly a decade later.

SUPPORTING THE NEXT GENERATION OF TEACHERS

If we want to do the best job we can at breaking down gender stereotypes in schools, we need to start with the people who will soon be leading classrooms of their own. That means thinking carefully about how we support our trainee teachers and making sure they're equipped not just to navigate gendered expectations, but to challenge them.

Back when we ran the survey discussed in Chapter 6, we asked a few extra questions about teacher training. Specifically, we wanted to know what kind of support male trainees had received and whether they felt more could be done during training to prepare them for the realities of primary teaching. The first question asked whether male trainees had received any kind of support specifically because they were men. A huge 92 per cent said no. For the 8 per cent who had received something, it tended to be brief and usually in the context of safeguarding. In other words, it was less about helping men feel prepared or valued and more about warning them to be cautious. Some quotes made that fairly clear:

- 'There were 12 males out of a course of 180. They got us all together and told us statistically we were more likely to fail and would need to take this seriously.'

- 'A lecture on being extra careful around children due to perceptions about men & kids.'

When asked whether they would have liked more support, 38 per cent said yes. Most struggled to say what that support would look like, but a few patterns emerged. Some wanted a male mentor – someone with lived experience who could offer advice and reassurance. Others wanted guidance on dealing with the assumptions people often make about men working with children, or practical discussions about things like 'safe touch' and professional boundaries. Overall, there was almost no appetite for special treatment but just a simple desire for a bit of guidance and for people to better understand what it's like to be a man entering a female-dominated profession. However, there was one comment that stuck out:

- 'Maybe the question should be what we could change about the training for all teachers?'

This comment suggests a wider hope that everyone, not just men, think harder about the gendered assumptions we all carry with us into the profession. In fact, the most common theme in response to our final survey question – 'what should training providers be doing more of?' – was simply to raise awareness. Men didn't want gender-specific modules or tokenistic workshops. They wanted more space in training to think about gender overall. That feels like a crucial point because, if we want to create schools that challenge stereotypes, we have to make sure the people stepping into the profession aren't bringing those same stereotypes in with them. Unfortunately, research suggests that they are.

A study by de Salis et al. (2018: 10) captured this conversation between two female trainee teachers:

F1: *Male trainees make better KS2 teachers.*

F3: *I've always thought that you know.*

F1: *I think it's because as boys get older they start getting a bit of attitude and all that and they need like a male role model … you know like Dads are often more strict, like they might try and be [like]…*

F3: *[I don't know], I think children see males as having more authority.*

The researchers were surprised by how widespread this kind of thinking still was among trainees. Many of their interviews contained traditional ideas about what men and women are naturally good at. For instance, female trainees spoke about men being better at discipline or handling older children and male trainees described themselves as better leaders. The authors pointed out how worrying it is that those training to teach are still holding on to gender-based myths.

We should care about this for two reasons. First, these ideas can influence how children in their future classes view themselves. And second, they shape how future teachers see themselves. If male trainees don't feel they're naturally suited to nurturing, for example, they're more likely to avoid working with younger children, or to avoid primary teaching altogether. And when men expect to lead, and women expect to care, we end up with the same leadership dynamics repeating themselves. That's why the authors argue that teacher training courses need to do more. Not by adding tokenistic lectures on gender, but by making sure that trainees are given opportunities to think about their own assumptions. As they put it, 'if trainee teachers have stereotypical self-images of themselves and their colleagues based on gender, it seems sensible and necessary to challenge these as part of training programmes' (de Salis et al. 2018: 12).

I appreciate that what I'm suggesting here is not easy to implement. Schools and training providers already have too much to cover and not enough time to cover it in. So what gets left out to make space for this? If awareness of gender stereotypes isn't a built-in part of the framework or curriculum, then it's often left more to choice. But my hope is that what I've shown here makes the case for why that choice is worth making, because this work of raising awareness is hugely important. It influences the kind of teachers we become, the messages we pass on to children and has the potential to change lives.

REFERENCES

Beckerman, H. (2018). 'Comedian Robert Webb on masculinity, making jokes and getting lost'. *Financial Times*, 27 April. Available at: www.ft.com/content/e9632932-4816-11e8-8ae9-4b5ddcca99b3 (accessed 6 May 2025).

de Salis, C., Rowley, A., Stokell, K., & Brundrett, M. (2018). 'Do we need more male primary teachers? Tensions and contradictions in the perspectives of male and female trainees'. *Education 3–13*, 47(1), 1–15. https://doi.org/10.1080/03004279.2018.1498997

Devlin, H., & Allegretti, A. (2022). 'Girls shun physics A-level as they dislike "hard maths", says social mobility head'. *The Guardian*, 27 April. Available at: www.theguardian.com/education/2022/apr/27/girls-shun-physics-a-level-as-they-dislike-hard-maths-says-social-mobility-head (accessed 6 May 2025).

Fawcett Society. (2020a). 'Unlimited potential: The final report of the Commission on Gender Stereotypes in Early Childhood'. Available at: www.fawcettsociety.org.uk/Handlers/Download.ashx?IDMF=17fb0c11-f904-469c-a62e-173583d441c8 (accessed 1 June 2025).

Fawcett Society. (2020b). 'Unlimited potential: The final report of the Commission on Gender Stereotypes in Early Childhood' [Summary]. Available at: www.fawcettsociety.org.uk/unlimited-potential-the-final-report-of-the-commission-on-gender-stereotypes-in-early-childhood (accessed 1 June 2025).

Gorard, S., & See, B. H. (2023). 'Why are so many graduates shunning teaching? Pay – but not bonuses – could be the answer'. *The Conversation*, 21 November. Available at: https://theconversation.com/why-are-so-many-graduates-shunning-teaching-pay-but-not-bonuses-could-be-the-answer-216963 (last accessed 6 May 2025).

Han, S. W., Borgonovi, F., & Guerriero, S. (2020). 'Why don't more boys want to become teachers? The effect of a gendered profession on students' career expectations'. *International Journal of Educational Research*, 103, 101645. https://doi.org/10.1016/j.ijer.2020.101645

Hares, S., Nagesh, R., & Konate, M. (2022). 'Was your teacher sexist? Teacher beliefs and students outcomes'. Center for Global Development. Available at: https://www.cgdev.org/blog/was-your-teacher-sexist-teacher-beliefs-and-students-outcomes. (accessed 6 May 2025).

Phys.org. (2021). 'Children's books may help solidify gender stereotypes at a young age'. Available at: https://phys.org/news/2021-12-children-solidify-gender-stereotypes-young.html (accessed 6 May 2025).

Rycroft-Smith, L., & Andre, G. (eds). (2019). *The Equal Classroom: Life-Changing Thinking About Gender*. London: Routledge.

Saujani, R. (2016). 'Teach girls bravery, not perfection' [Blog post, 8 March]. Medium. Available at: https://medium.com/@reshmasaujani/teach-girls-bravery-not-perfection-257691d13476 (accessed 6 May 2025).

Warin, J. (2017). 'Conceptualising the value of male practitioners in early childhood education and care: gender balance or gender flexibility'. *Gender and Education*, 31(3), 293–308. https://doi.org/10.1080/09540253.2017.1380172

Webb, R. (2017). 'Robert Webb: "I was never very good at being a boy"'. *The Guardian*, 20 August. Available at: https://www.theguardian.com/books/2017/aug/20/robert-webb-autobiography-how-not-to-be-a-boy-peep-show (accessed 6 May 2025).

Yates, K. (2022, June 21). 'So, Katharine Birbalsingh – girls do like hard maths after all. Well, well'. *The Independent*, 21 June. Available at: https://www.independent.co.uk/voices/katharine-birbalsingh-hard-maths-girls-stem-b2105888.html (accessed 6 May 2025).

14

RETHINKING RECRUITMENT: A CONVERSATION WITH CLAUDIO SISERA

Our work is not just about placing men in jobs; it's about fostering a supportive, inclusive environment where they can succeed and, in turn, help reshape the future of education.

(C. Sisera, personal communication, 12 August 2024)

INTRODUCTION

Running the MTP network has given us a small but valuable window into the world of teacher recruitment, including two opportunities to speak with the DfE. The first of these conversations, in 2020, came about after they became aware of the stories of men in primary we were sharing. This meeting was an opportunity to share ideas and information, but no more than that. By the time of our second conversation, in late 2022, recruitment was at the top of the agenda. At the time, in a post-pandemic world of increasing 'work from home' opportunities, there was growing national concern about missed recruitment targets. For years, several secondary subjects had faced chronic shortages of teachers, but now primary education was also falling short. At the time, the low numbers prompted Geoff Barton, General Secretary of the Association of School and College Leaders, to declare that 'trainee teacher recruitment has plumbed new depths' (Martin, 2023).

At government level, state education seemed increasingly rudderless. In 2022 alone, there were four education secretaries. And while the national picture was concerning, the challenges closer to home felt even more disheartening. Some of the MTP network's strongest early advocates – men who had once passionately written about the privilege and joy of teaching – were stepping away from the profession. Everything was beginning to feel a little out of control and it became harder and harder to push for gender balance in teaching when the profession itself seemed to be unravelling.

But amidst this rather bleak landscape, I came across Claudio Sisera and his work. His approach to recruitment stood out as both refreshing and effective. Instead of focusing on the systemic challenges we all know exist, Claudio's network seemed to ask a different question: how do we bring men into education in a way that works right now? I first encountered his organisation, Male Childcare & Teaching Jobs, on social media. It was impossible to miss. Its design was professional, its messaging positive and its articles and webinars insightful. At that point, I was already in the process of writing this book and I knew I needed to talk to him. I messaged Claudio, introduced myself, and asked if he'd be willing to share his story and approach. This chapter is the result of that conversation.

LET'S START AT THE BEGINNING - WHAT DREW YOU TO WORKING WITH CHILDREN?

I grew up in a small town about half an hour's drive from Naples, Italy. My early years were marked by the familiar rhythms of southern Italian life. School during the year followed by summer jobs to gain a sense of financial independence. In Italy, we enjoy three months of summer holidays between June and September, which I spent working as a lifeguard at a local outdoor swimming pool. This routine continued until I finished secondary school at the age of 19. At that crossroads, I faced a decision. To attend university, apply for a state job or move abroad. Limited opportunities in Italy led me to explore life beyond my small town. With the encouragement of friends who had ventured overseas, I decided to move to the UK, drawn by the allure of London, a cosmopolitan city teeming with opportunities and diverse cultures. It was a leap into the unknown, but one that promised new experiences and professional growth that I couldn't foresee in Italy.

Arriving in London at 19, I had no clear career path in mind. I stayed with a friend for the first two weeks, during which I pounded the pavements with a stack of CVs, applying for any job I could find – from waitering to receptionist roles. My 'big break' came in an unexpected way when my friend's flatmate, a room leader at a nursery in Fulham, asked if I'd ever considered working in childcare. With no experience to speak of, I was hesitant, but the offer of an apprenticeship, along with the pressing need to find a job quickly, pushed me to give it a try. I still remember that first interview – understanding very little of what was said due to the language barrier, yet somehow securing the job.

Initially, I struggled to see childcare as a long-term career and often felt out of place. My colleagues would occasionally make light-hearted comments about my work, particularly when I engaged in tasks traditionally seen as feminine, like bottle-feeding or cleaning up after the children. These moments were compounded by some parents' discomfort, such as when one requested that I not change their daughter's nappy. I often felt like an outsider, more at home discussing football or gaming than the topics that dominated the staff room. There were times when I even found relief in being pulled out of the classroom to carry delivery boxes – any excuse to escape a situation where I didn't quite fit in.

However, things began to change after I earned my Level 3 qualification. My manager, recognising something in me that I hadn't yet seen in myself, asked if I would cover for the room leader during her maternity leave. This opportunity became a turning point. Suddenly, I felt needed and valued. I realised that I could bring my own approach to the classroom, shaping activities and fostering a more inclusive and judgement-free environment. What began as a temporary position quickly turned into a permanent role. And, as the nursery transitioned to new ownership, I seized the additional training opportunities, rapidly progressing to the nursery manager's position. This experience gave me the confidence to start my own nursery, Little Green Steps, built on an ethos of sustainability. And this became the foundation of my career in childcare. It was a path I never planned to take, but one that has shaped my life profoundly.

WHAT IMPACT DID THE PANDEMIC HAVE?

The onset of COVID-19 couldn't have come at a worse time for my business. Just two weeks after investing heavily in new premises to accommodate a growing waiting list at my early years setting, everything came to a standstill. The economic fallout forced many parents to reduce or withdraw their children's attendance. The once-promising waiting list began to dwindle, leaving me with no option but to close down. It was a devastating blow, not just to the business but also to my sense of direction. I found myself at another crossroads, uncertain about my next steps. Returning to work in other nurseries felt unappealing, especially with the restrictive measures in place – bubbles, limited attendance and curtailed learning activities all seemed to stifle the very essence of what early years education should be.

So, I took a leap of faith and decided to pursue an apprenticeship in digital marketing – a decision that came with significant financial sacrifices, but one that allowed me to expand my skillset. This period of transition also opened up new avenues for me. I began to network more extensively, connecting with educators and leaders beyond the confines of my previous nursery walls. It was during these interactions that I noticed common patterns among the men I encountered in the industry. The challenges I had faced early in my career – feeling isolated, undervalued and out of place – were echoed in their stories. This realisation pushed me to dig deeper, researching the benefits of a gender-balanced teaching workforce and the barriers men face in the field. While the presence of men in early years education brings undeniable benefits, there was a huge lack of support to make this a reality.

This became the foundation for Male Childcare & Teaching Jobs. I wanted it to be more than just a recruitment platform. It had to be a comprehensive resource, rooted in diversity, equity and inclusion (DEI), with a mission to challenge and transform gender dynamics in education. Our approach would focus not only on recruitment but also on creating gender-inclusive environments through policy implementation, professional development and community building. Early on, we encountered scepticism and market resistance, but we also discovered a passionate community of men eager to support our cause.

WHAT MAKES YOUR RECRUITMENT MODEL DIFFERENT FROM TRADITIONAL APPROACHES?

Our recruitment model is meticulously designed to address the unique challenges of encouraging men to pursue careers in education and caregiving. We've developed a strategy that combines collaboration, targeted outreach and strategic partnerships to find and select the right candidates for educational institutions. We begin by collaborating with educational institutions – schools, colleges, and universities – to promote teaching careers among men. By hosting information sessions and career guidance events, we reach potential candidates early in their decision-making process. These sessions not only highlight the rewards of a career in education but also provide a platform for direct engagement with male students who might not have previously considered this path.

Our targeted outreach programmes are carefully crafted to reach men who may be interested in teaching but are unsure how to proceed or are put off by societal stereotypes. Using a variety of channels – social media, community events and online platforms – we challenge existing stereotypes and offer a clear, inspiring picture of what a career in teaching can offer. By showcasing real-life examples of men thriving in education, we help break down barriers and encourage more men to consider this rewarding career. In addition to outreach, we actively participate in and organise career fairs. These events provide valuable opportunities for men to explore teaching and connect directly with employers. It also allows us to engage with men who are considering a transition into education, offering them personalised guidance and addressing any concerns they might have. These interactions are vital in helping potential candidates understand the support and mentorship available to them through our organisation.

To further extend our reach, we establish partnerships with men's charities and organisations. These collaborations are key in connecting us with men from diverse backgrounds who may not traditionally consider a career in education but possess the qualities and passion needed to excel as educators. Through these partnerships, we offer ongoing support and mentorship, guiding these individuals towards fulfilling careers in teaching.

HOW DO YOU ENSURE THE CANDIDATES YOU RECRUIT ARE THE RIGHT FIT FOR THE SCHOOLS AND SETTINGS THEY JOIN, AND HOW DO YOU SUPPORT THEM IN THEIR ROLES?

We assess candidates not only on their qualifications but also on their passion for education and their commitment to creating inclusive, supportive environments. This process includes interviews, background checks and practical assessments where appropriate. We work closely with our clients – nurseries, schools, recruitment agencies and apprenticeship providers – to understand their specific needs and ensure that the candidates we place are not only technically qualified but also a good fit for the institutions.

And for the candidates themselves, we offer ongoing training, mentorship and professional development opportunities to ensure they are well-prepared for their roles. Our team of mentors is a key component of our support framework. Each mentor specialises in a different aspect of education, offering tailored guidance to suit the unique needs of our candidates. From leadership and management to apprenticeships, neurodivergence and safeguarding, their expertise covers a wide spectrum of challenges educators may face. These mentors not only provide practical advice, but also act as models of success, demonstrating how men can thrive in this profession. And, in addition to this, we run monthly webinars where topics are chosen by our community members, ensuring that the content we deliver is directly relevant to their needs. Our organisation sources passionate male experts in various fields to lead these sessions, providing our audience with relatable male mentoring figures who can inspire and guide them.

CAN YOU TELL ME ABOUT SOME OF THE MENTORS AND HOW THEIR BACKGROUNDS ENRICH THE SUPPORT THEY PROVIDE?

Our mentorship team is the cornerstone of our approach. Here, in their own words, are the stories of two of them.

David Wright - Mentor for Fathers

I met my future wife at a party in my home city of Southampton in my last year studying economics at University College London. On graduating, we returned to marry and live in Southampton where I pursued a career in IT for the next 25 years. My wife, already qualified as an NNEB nursery nurse, was unable to secure employment in the early years sector at that time due to lack of opportunity because there were so few early years providers in the area. Following the birth of our children, my wife started a preschool in our home, which eventually outgrew both the space and demand for longer hours. This led to a move to a dedicated building, marking the beginning of Paint Pots Nurseries.

I joined when it had grown to two day nurseries. As an IT technician, I had become disenchanted with the politics and demands of the management role I eventually found myself in, within a large organisation where I did not feel I mattered or made a difference, and the future of my job role was uncertain. My wife and I shared a passion for making a difference in children's lives and we wanted to work together. I retrained, acquiring a level 3 NVQ in childcare followed by Early Years Professional Status. I worked directly with the children for several years before taking on the role of manager of a setting.

My wife and I eventually oversaw strategy and operations across the organisation, before retiring in 2022, 30 years after Paint Pots was established and 18 years after I joined. We both continue to support both Paint Pots (which, as of 2024, has expanded to 13 sites) and other settings with training and consultancy alongside some writing and occasional speaking engagements. We also work voluntarily for several charities and organisations focused on supporting the early years sector, families and children, in the UK and globally.

Karl Eaveson – Mentor for Students

My story is a common one I hear among the male Early Years community. When I was a teenager, I had an interest in working with children but didn't pursue this when I left school at 16. Instead, I began working as a baker for a well-known company alongside studying to become an electrician. But after a few years, I realised I was unhappy and that I needed to change something. After some research into working with children, I took the leap and enrolled on a two-day introduction to childcare course through Scarborough Council, and the rest, as they say, is history. Fourteen years later, I am loving my career and can't wait to go to work each day.

In Early Years, you witness so many wonderful 'firsts'. The first steps, first mumbled 'bye byes,' the first time on the potty. When children accomplish something, it makes you beam with pride. I honestly believe that the day I don't feel this anymore, then it is time for a change. My average day varies but as part of my role as Nursery Manager in my current setting, I spend up to three-quarters of my working week working in the rooms with the children and supporting the teams on the floor. I also spend focus periods with each individual room to support and guide the practitioners and document progress so we can see how things are progressing week to week.

BASED ON WHAT YOU'VE LEARNED, WHAT ADVICE WOULD YOU GIVE TO DIFFERENT STAKEHOLDERS WHO WANT TO SUPPORT GENDER DIVERSITY IN EDUCATION?

To create meaningful change, *everyone* must play their part in fostering an inclusive environment that attracts and supports male educators. We must move beyond awareness and into action. Here are three strategies that can help support progress.

1   Cultivate a supportive culture that tells men 'you belong here'.

    a   Review leave policies – are new fathers given equal access to parental leave and are they encouraged to do so? Is flexible work positioned as a valid option for all staff?

    b   Add a gender-inclusive statement to the staff handbook and recruitment packs.

    c   Run workshops that consider how staff can unintentionally reinforce gender stereotypes in the classroom through use of gendered language and to interrogate the hidden messages in the resources used.

    d   Review where and how you advertise roles to ensure recruitment efforts widen the pool of applicants, but always prioritise the best candidate for the role.

2   Make gender diversity a priority.

    a   Embed gender diversity as part of strategic planning within the school development plan. During recruitment cycles, ask 'Have we done everything reasonable to attract a diverse applicant pool?'

    b   Ask important questions about the diversity of school teams and governance itself. Are the teams representative of the families and communities they serve? We have not had a male teacher or TA in over three years – why might that be?

3   Facilitate collaboration to share what works.

    a   Informally collaborate with other nurseries, schools and educational networks to share best practices for recruiting and retaining male educators.

    b   Or create a more structured 'working group' to create shared resources (example job adverts, one page do/don'ts for male recruitment) and trial different approaches and report back.

WHAT ARE SOME KEY QUESTIONS THAT INSTITUTIONS, EDUCATORS AND INDIVIDUALS CAN ASK THEMSELVES TO REFLECT ON AND CONTRIBUTE TO IMPROVING GENDER DIVERSITY IN EDUCATION?

Consider how the following questions might apply to your own institution and how they could inform your future strategies. Some may be more applicable to early years settings where the numbers of men are very low.

1 Team Diversity

How diverse is your current staff and what steps have you taken to promote gender diversity? Could your policies better support and include male educators?

2 Recruitment Policies

Are your recruitment strategies effectively reaching a diverse pool of candidates, including men? How could these efforts be innovated to attract more male educators?

3 Retention and Support

What systems are in place to ensure male educators feel valued, supported and connected? Could additional resources or initiatives strengthen their sense of belonging?

4 Mentorship and Career Development

Do you offer mentorship programmes tailored to male educators' needs? How could these programmes or professional development opportunities better support their growth?

5 Community and Parental Engagement

How does your institution engage with parents and the community to challenge stereotypes? Could schools work more closely with local fathers – perhaps through school events, volunteering, mentoring or governance – and in doing so, make primary schools feel more welcoming to men generally, potentially improving gender representation in the long term?

6 Vision for Gender Diversity

What does success look like for your institution in achieving gender diversity? How will you measure progress and what milestones will signal you're on the right track?

Claudio's recruitment model offers an interesting case study in addressing the challenges of gender diversity in education. While his approach specifically focuses on men in early years, the overall model reflects the main themes explored in this book: the importance of both attracting and retaining a wider range of people and creating environments where they can thrive. His model goes beyond recruitment, recognising the crucial role of mentorship, professional development and workplace culture in supporting educators once they are through the door. This is important because, although not an issue for some men, we have seen throughout this book that many male educators experience feelings of social isolation or the pressure to conform to traditional gender roles. By addressing these challenges holistically, Claudio's work provides an example of how targeted recruitment can lead to meaningful and sustainable change.

That being said, this chapter is not intended to prescribe a singular solution or suggest that this model is the only path forward. Some readers may question whether focusing on one demographic group is the right approach, and those reservations are fair.

However, this chapter does not serve to provide definitive answers but to present innovative ideas and invite discussion. I've chosen to highlight Claudio's work because it offers a different perspective: one based on a genuine commitment to supporting male educators and building inclusive, long-term approaches to gender diversity in the workforce.

REFERENCES

Martin, M. (2023). 'Revealed: Secondary ITT target missed by half: government data shows the teacher recruitment crisis has "plumbed new depths", heads' leaders warn'. *Tes Magazine*, 7 December. Available at: www.tes.com/magazine/news/general/teacher-trainee-recruitment-itt-target-missed-half (accessed 18 May 2025).

CONCLUSION

With toxic online influences on the rise, our boys need strong, positive male role models to look up to. At home, of course, and at school too… So I want more male teachers – teaching, guiding, leading the boys in their classrooms.

(Bridget Phillipson, as quoted in Adams, 2025)

INTRODUCTION

Right at the point where I was finishing this book – proofreading the chapters, checking references, doing all those final polishes before submission – people started talking about a new Netflix drama called *Adolescence*. It's that sort of series that suddenly everyone's watching and talking about. There are opinion pieces in every paper and social media is full of it. It is the must-watch show of the year and the kind that is bound to win all the awards.

It tells the story of a 13-year-old boy, Jamie Miller, who murders a 13-year-old girl. According to one of the leads, Stephen Graham, it's not a whodunit, it's a *whydunit*. Across four episodes, all filmed in single takes, the show investigates what led a young boy in Britain to such violence. It looks at his home life, his school life and the influences around him. And, to be fair, it is brilliant. The acting is extraordinary and the cinematography is special. As a piece of television, it is incredibly well made. But it is a fictional drama.

I had a feeling, as the conversation started picking up, that it would very quickly shift. That public and media discussion would turn into political discussion. Within days, it did. The drama was no longer just a drama. It became a story about *the* modern teenage boy in Britain and Jamie Miller became a symbol of toxic masculinity. And having spent over a year researching and writing this book, I knew exactly what would come next.

A week later, the above quote from Bridget Phillipson, Secretary of State for Education, was headlining multiple newspapers. Suddenly, the conversation wasn't just about one boy. It was about all boys. And we were back to that same narrative, the one I explored in Chapter 9. Boys in crisis. And with it, a familiar solution that we need more male teachers to serve as role models. Phillipson joins a long line of education secretaries who have, often with good intentions but not always with evidence, offered this as part of the answer. It was a predictable knee-jerk response to a much more complicated issue. But it also shows how quickly the subject of male teachers can become topical again and how emotional and reactive the conversation can be.

When Matt and I first started Men Teach Primary, it wasn't with an agenda or any long-term plan. It was just a way to connect with others during a time of isolation.

We didn't set out to solve the problem; we just wanted to talk about it. And I suppose that's what this book has been too – a way of talking about something that's always been there, but rarely explored with much real depth. I hope the book has offered a fuller picture of what it means to be a man in primary. But more than that, I hope it has helped show why having more men teaching our children is a good thing and something worth working towards. Back in Chapter 1, I explained how one of my earliest realisations was that this book had to be more than just making a stronger case for having more men in primary teaching. It had to paint a fuller picture of why so few men choose the profession and what their presence or absence *really* means. At that point, I shared a set of big ideas that helped to frame the story. Now, as we reach the end, I want to return to that approach. What follows is a set of final thoughts I've been left with through the process of writing. There's no single answer to the debate around men in primary education, but I hope these ideas offer something useful as a way to help us have more informed conversations going forward.

1 WE MUST STOP MAKING THE CASE FOR MORE MEN USING FLAWED ARGUMENTS

We've heard them all before and, as we have seen above, they keep being repeated: that men are better at discipline; that boys will do better in school if they've got a man at the front of the room; that men can step in to fill a gap in boys' lives. They rely on tired stereotypes, undervalue the incredible work done by women, and distract us from what really matters: great teaching. Being male isn't a shortcut to being good at this job. It never has been and never should be. If we want more of the right people in classrooms, we need to move on from these myths and focus on what really improves children's lives.

2 WE NEED TO RETHINK WHAT WE MEAN BY 'ROLE MODEL'

This is the argument people find hardest to let go of and I understand why. Of course men can be role models. But so can women. So can anyone. The problem is when we start using 'male role model' as an umbrella term for a particular kind of masculinity: someone to toughen boys up, to stand in for absent dads and to bring good 'old fashioned' discipline into the classroom. That's a huge pressure to put on one person and it's far too narrow. The most powerful role modelling male teachers can do is to show that care, kindness and emotional intelligence aren't gendered. Just by being themselves, doing the job well and being visible, they can challenge old ideas about what men can be.

3 WE NEED TO RECOGNISE HOW SOCIETAL ATTITUDES STILL STRONGLY INFLUENCE WHAT WE THINK MEN AND WOMEN ARE GOOD AT

Of course men and women aren't the same but a huge part of what we see as 'difference' is shaped by our gendered world. The way we're raised, what we're praised for and the expectations placed on us. Primary teaching is still seen by many as 'women's work'. Not because women are better at it, but because we've been conditioned to believe that they are. These messages come from everywhere. And what's hardest is when those same beliefs come from within the profession itself. If we want to change that, schools have to lead the way by dismantling gender stereotypes. Because if we keep falling back on old assumptions about what men and women are 'naturally' good at, we'll never break the cycle of job segregation.

4 WE CAN'T TALK ABOUT MEN IN PRIMARY WITHOUT TALKING ABOUT WOMEN TOO

This book may be about men in primary, but it's not a campaign for men to replace women or take the spotlight. Women have built this profession and their work (often undervalued and underpaid) has kept schools going for decades. If we care about equity, we all need to keep talking about working conditions, equal pay and leadership access. For example, why is it that in a profession overwhelmingly made up of women, maternity conditions still lag behind so many other sectors? The recent 'Missing Mothers' report revealed that women in their 30s are the single biggest group leaving teaching, with more than 9,000 women leaving teaching in England 2022–23, compared with just over 3,400 men of a similar age (Jeffreys, 2024). Why have we made it so hard for mothers to stay in the classroom? So, the conversation about men in primary should never be a case of men versus women but about creating a profession where everyone feels respected, supported and able to thrive.

5 WE KNOW THIS IS NOT THE FULL STORY THERE'S MORE TO EXPLORE

There are areas I would have liked to explore further. The scope of this book meant making some difficult choices about what to include and what to leave for another time. I'd planned to speak to teenage boys and listen to their perceptions of primary teaching. I'd hoped to look more closely at university training routes and speak to those working directly with trainee teachers. I wanted to explore the power of male mentorship and peer networks in more depth. I also accept that, for clarity, this book has sometimes referred to men as a single group. But of course, men's experiences in education are shaped by many other parts of their identity – race, sexuality, class, disability and more. These intersections bring specific challenges, pressures and stories that deserve deeper exploration than this book was able to give. My hope is that future work continues to build on this conversation.

6 WE NEED TO DECIDE WHAT KIND OF PROFESSION WE WANT

Writing this book has forced me to keep coming back to a bigger question, not just about men in primary, but about the workforce as a whole. Because, even if we could recruit more men into primary teaching, it would not fix the wider problem: we are struggling to build and sustain a strong and experienced workforce. The real challenge is keeping teachers in our schools. We are losing far too many, far too soon. At the time of writing, tens of thousands of teachers are sharing career alternatives in online communities designed for those leaving the profession. That's thousands of years of experience and expertise leaving our schools and probably not coming back. Not because those teachers didn't care but because the system made it too difficult for them to continue. As I argued in Chapter 13, making teaching a rewarding and sustainable career option has to be the foundation for any progress. Without that bedrock, efforts to strengthen or diversify the workforce simply won't last.

In 2019, the DfE's Recruitment and Retention Strategy recognised many of the right issues, particularly around workload, early-career support and professional development. However, the educational landscape has changed since then. Post-Covid pressures around attendance and behaviour, the growing complexity of additional needs and a high-stakes inspection system have left many schools operating in a constant state of survival mode. The demands on teachers keep rising, yet the specialist support around them has not kept pace.

All of this affects how the job feels day to day. Teachers routinely give more than they're paid for. They work weekends, evenings and holidays. Not because they're told to, but because the job is so all consuming and because they care. But we cannot continue relying on goodwill. It's not sustainable and it's not fair. If we want people to stay in teaching for longer, we have to make the job worth staying in.

I'm sometimes asked what I would be doing if I weren't a teacher. And even when the job frustrates me, as it so often does, I never have an answer. Because I can't think of anything better. Teaching lets me use my brain; be creative; work alongside kind, passionate people; and make a difference in my community. That's rare and it's special. But it's also such a tough job at times that sometimes you forget how special it is. And I'm not saying the job should be easy – the most important jobs never are. But it should be more manageable and it should be something that more children grow up dreaming of doing.

My youngest daughter often lines up her toys and teaches them reading or maths (and occasionally threatens them with a sanction for misbehaviour), copying the wonderful teachers she's had. She tells me proudly, 'I'm going to be a teacher like Daddy.' It's great to hear. I love that she sees the joy and purpose in what I do. And if she does follow this path, she'd be the fourth generation in our family to teach primary, following in the footsteps of her Great Granda. I'd be so proud if she did. But more than anything, I hope she steps into a profession that's better than the one we have now because the thought of that enthusiasm being quickly worn away is heartbreaking.

What happens next isn't down to one of us. It's down to all of us educators, leaders, policymakers and parents to decide what kind of education system we want to build. At the heart of that system is the workforce. If we want brilliant teachers of any gender to choose this profession and stay in it, then we have to make it a career that is sustainable and gets the respect it deserves. If we get that right, then *everyone* benefits.

REFERENCES

Adams, R. (2025). 'We need more male teachers so British boys have role models, says minister'. *The Guardian*, 3 April. Available at: www.theguardian.com/education/2025/apr/03/bridget-phillipson-education-secretary-more-male-teachers-adolescence (accessed 18 May 2025).

Jeffreys, B. (2024). 'Teacher mums who leave profession fuelling shortages'. BBC News, 2 August. Available at: https://www.bbc.co.uk/news/articles/c51yzv95wg9o (accessed 18 May 2025).

INDEX

INDEX

Inge Bosse

Wo
ist der
Hut?

**LAUTER
VERLAG**